THE MEAT LOVER'S
SLOW COOKER
COOKBOOK

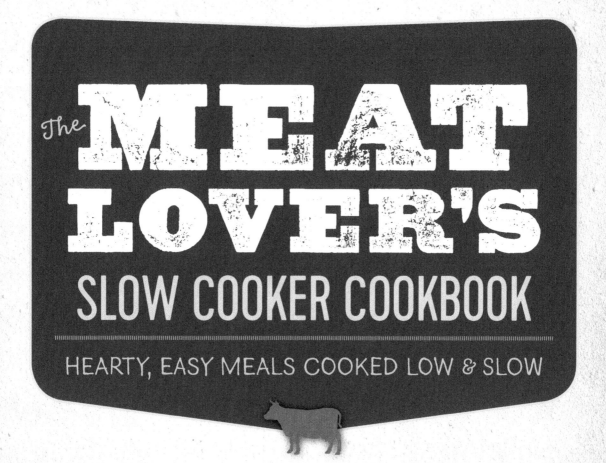

The MEAT LOVER'S SLOW COOKER COOKBOOK

HEARTY, EASY MEALS COOKED LOW & SLOW

Jennifer Olvera

SONOMA
PRESS

To Mike, my steadfast partner and best friend,
and Hayden, my son, for inspiring me every day;
you both, time and time again,
have motivated and pushed me to the finish line.

CONTENTS

INTRODUCTION

*I*t started with pork paprikash. You could call it my gateway slow cooker recipe —tested at a time when I was professionally developing recipes at a rapid-fire rate. I'd been making various versions of paprikash on my stovetop for years, and they were great. Fantastic, actually. But my interest in slow cooking was beginning to catapult, and I never shied away from a cooking challenge. That's when I started moving some recipes to the crock—a kitchen tool that has since become an indispensable staple.

After pork paprikash it was Sunday gravy. Then beef stew, followed shortly by chicken tortilla soup. I was determined to test the range of the slow cooker—and to turn out winning dishes with complex flavors on a Tuesday or Thursday night. Moreover, these happened to be our favorite suppers. I found I could make them more effortlessly in the slow cooker, in a way that worked with my hectic schedule. These slow cooker versions were not only unbelievably convenient—their flavors were unbeatable.

But, to be completely honest, before I was commissioned to develop slow cooker recipes for various publications, I didn't give the appliance all that much thought. During my formative cooking years, I'd tried various recipes and they often tasted the same, flat. I've always prided myself on having an adventuresome palate that demands a range of flavors, cuisines, textures, and inspirations. So I was pleased to learn that, as I experimented more with the slow cooker, many of those requirements actually could be met separate of the stove. Ultimately, meat ended up being key and everything else supported it.

When cooked in the slow cooker, these tasty, tender, and filling meals are an easy way to get dinner on the table, often with leftovers to spare. Leftovers are something I depend on, since being a mom to a 12-year-old baseball player always has me on the move. Featuring minimal preparation time, familiar ingredients, and full-flavor results that await you at the end of the day, these recipes have been written to make it easy to get a home-cooked meal on the table every night of the week.

Of course, I'm not the first person to sing the praises of the slow cooker. These days, slow cooker recipes are everywhere and options are seemingly endless. But when it comes to making slow cooker meals and sides with great results, time and time again, what I found missing is a compilation of the very best recipes. I put this cookbook together for those looking for go-to recipes they can count on, rather than an exhaustive collection of slow cooker inspiration. If you share meals made from this cookbook with neighbors and friends, prepare yourself for recipe requests—it might even get annoying.

After years of slow cooking, pot roast remains a personal favorite, my Mexican Pot Roast (page 51) in particular. My recipe for Barbacoa (page 56), which my son never ceases to request, also transitioned effortlessly to the slow cooker. Without a slow cooker, I would never even attempt cooking the extra-leisurely Hawaiian-Style Kalua Pig (page 97)—unless, of course, a pit magically appears in my backyard one day.

Other recipes remind me of childhood, like the Chicken and Dumplings (page 127), and the Cheesy Creamed Corn with Bacon (page 160), which is an update on the canned stuff I'll sheepishly admit I still have an affinity for.

I see this one-pot cooking appliance as a reason to revamp Sunday supper favorites for everyday enjoyment, knowing I don't have to be in the kitchen to oversee them. Whether you favor a rich marinara, crave hearty beef-vegetable soup, or want to prepare pork shoulder for company, you'll find what you need in the pages that follow. You get to decide what suits you. And you can use these recipes as a springboard for your own creations—I encourage that. There are no hard-to-find ingredients here, just straightforward crowd pleasers that require minimal effort but deliver maximum flavor.

1
FAVORITE MEALS COOKED SLOW

I LOVE A GOOD SLOW-COOKED

meal, be it chicken and dumplings, savory pot roast, or hearty Italian gravy. The problem is, I don't always have time to stir and fuss over the stove while I have deadlines to adhere to, a son to care for, a garden to weed, places to go, and people to see. That's why the slow cooker is a fixture in my kitchen. My take? It should be a fixture in yours, too. With that in mind, you'll find family-friendly recipes in the chapters that follow, alongside updated and globally influenced main courses. All are here to tempt your taste buds while providing you with an incentive to skip the drive-thru—even on the busiest of days. Each recipe has a handful of things in common: it's meat-minded, nutritious, easy-to-prepare, and full of flavorful zing. Plus (and this is the whole idea), it'll leave you with more time to enjoy the company of loved ones.

MEAT'S BEST FRIEND

Budget friendly, energy efficient, and easy to use, the slow cooker—more than the pressure cooker, oven, or even the Dutch oven—is meat's best friend, transforming inexpensive cuts into company-worthy affairs.

As you likely know, slow cookers are electric pots that consist of a base with a heating element, a stoneware insert for even heat distribution, and a tight-fitting lid. The appliance works by trapping heat, and it evenly cooks dishes at relatively low temperatures for up to 10 hours without the evaporation of liquids that occurs in the oven or on the stove top. You're not *supposed* to mess with them. Rather, they're meant to be left unattended so the precious steam that cooks your meal doesn't escape. That lets you off the hook. Further adding to their appeal, there's some wiggle room with the cook time (slow cookers are pretty forgiving, after all).

WET AND WONDERFUL

The slow cooker employs a wet cooking method, relying on steam and consistent, relatively low heat. It's intended for cuts of meat that benefit from longer cooking times, so it's particularly suited to braises, soups, and stews, as well as sauces, stocks, hard vegetables, and grains.

Of course, some dishes actually aren't ideal candidates for long cooking. It's important to know which are and which aren't so you can ensure your slow-cooked dinner is ready, not ruined, at the end of the day. Rice and pasta, for example, become mushy. Tender cuts such as beef or pork tenderloin end up dry and tough. Seafood cooks quickly so the seafood recipes in this book use a different slow cooker approach and are more suited to cooking when you're at home. As for dairy, overcooking can cause it to either clump or separate. Other long-cooking no-nos include delicate veggies such as asparagus or peas.

So skip using tender meats entirely. The slow cooker solution for pasta, rice, seafood, dairy, and certain veggies is to be mindful of when you add them: shortly before serving.

Among the biggest attributes of the slow cooker is the rich flavor it helps create. This is the result of the ingredients simmering in their own juices at a low, steady temperature, creating deeply satisfying, zesty meals.

To make things even easier, you can throw everything into the stoneware bowl, cover it, and refrigerate the ingredients the night before. First thing in the morning, let the food in the bowl reach room temperature and then set it to cook. At the day's end, you'll be rewarded with a healthy, delicious, affordable meal—no matter how many to-dos you're juggling that day.

EVERY FAMILY'S SIDEKICK

There's no overstating what a workhorse the slow cooker is in the kitchen. But do you know how this hardworking appliance got its start?

Its history dates back to 1936, when Jewish inventor Irving Naxon found a new way to cook his mother's *cholent*—a long-cooking bean stew— while still observing the prohibition of working on the Sabbath. His patented Naxon Beanery All-Purpose Cooker featured an insert held by a casing that had a heating device to facilitate the even heating of food. The Rival Company later acquired and then reintroduced Naxon's bean cooker, under the brand name Crock-Pot. But it wasn't until 1974 that the bona fide Crock-Pot—the one with the removable stoneware insert we know today—made its debut.

At a time when more and more women were working outside the home, the appliance quickly grew in popularity. The Crock-Pot—marketed as a time-saver for working women—continued to sell like hotcakes through the 1970s. After that, a decade or two passed when enthusiasm for the slow cooker seemed to wane, most likely taking a temporary backseat to the microwave and the countless "time-saving" cooking products that quickly appeared and just as quickly disappeared.

Since 2000, the slow cooker has undergone a resurgence. In addition to its long-prized time-saving feature, there are many other benefits of slow cooking. Here are some of the most notable ones:

- **OFFERS A HEALTHY APPROACH** to cooking homemade meals made from scratch, ones that preserve nutrients and make it easy to cook whole foods

- **SAVES MONEY** since you can buy and transform less-expensive cuts of meat as well as buy ingredients in bulk and prepare multiple portions for the freezer

- **REDUCES ENERGY CONSUMPTION** given they use less than an oven

- **ENSURES EASY CLEANUP**, especially if you use a plastic insert or aluminum foil in the crock

SLOW COOKER OR CROCK-POT— WHAT'S THE DIFFERENCE?

Slow cooker is the generic name for an appliance that has heating elements in a metal housing around an insert and can be safely left unattended on your countertop as it slowly cooks a meal. *Crock-Pot* is the Rival Company's registered trademark for its slow cookers. The terms *slow cooker* and *Crock-Pot* are often used interchangeably, much like *tissue* and *Kleenex*. While all Crock-Pots are slow cookers, not all slow cookers are Crock-Pots. Other popular slow cooker brands include All-Clad, Cuisinart, and Hamilton Beach. Even the popular Instant Pot pressure cooker has a slow cooker function.

Slow cookers can be especially nice to use in the hot summer months when you want to avoid heating the oven (and your house), or adding to your energy bill. The appliance works through trapped low heat and steam, which has two benefits: The liquid and the nutrients can't escape, and the low temperature prevents the nutrients from breaking down. Once the lid goes on, you can safely leave the kitchen, and even the house. After the meal, the slow cooker stoneware insert can go straight into the dishwasher along with the dinner dishes.

THE RIGHT COOKER FOR YOU

Shopping for a new slow cooker can be a bit intimidating. The options are plentiful and the features really vary. All slow cookers have two heat settings: low (about 170°F) and high (usually 280°F). The bells and whistles go from there. Finding the right cooker for you depends on many factors, such as how and when you'll use it, your budget, and your family size. Before making a purchase, you should also consider the dishes you'll cook, and if you'll want leftovers. Learning a little about what's out there will also help with your decision.

SIZE

Among the most important choices you'll make when it comes to a slow cooker is its size. They range from a 1-quart cooker intended for dips, to a 2- to 6-quart home-meal version, to a party-ready 8-quart vessel. The 2-quart slow cooker is useful for just one or two servings, while a 6-quart cooker—the recommended size for recipes in this book—is large enough to accommodate a roast, feed a family of six, and (possibly) leave you with leftovers for the next day. Meanwhile, the 8-quart version can handle meals for 10 or more people, making it a great option for parties and anyone who likes to double recipes for the freezer.

SHAPE

The shape—round or oval—is more important than you might think. Do you mostly make soups, stews, and beans? Do you plan on keeping it on your counter? If so, a round one may be the best choice for you. If you plan on making roasts, whole chickens, brisket or ribs, then an oval slow cooker provides a better fit. (Of course, there is no rule that says you can't have more than one slow cooker.)

FEATURES

Typically, slow cookers come with a removable ceramic or porcelain insert, which makes for even heat distribution and easy cleaning. If you're in the market for a new slow cooker, look for one with a heating unit that rests not just at the bottom of the base but also goes up the side of the housing. This design affords the most even heat distribution. Avoid versions featuring a crock that simply sits atop the base, and particularly

THE GREAT BROWNING DEBATE

One of the great draws of the slow cooker is cooking in a single pot. For some slow cooker enthusiasts, any precooking defeats the purpose of the appliance. For others (and I'm in this camp), most meat that isn't browned first isn't worth eating.

There is no ultimate truth. The easiest option is to skip browning. And certain cuts of veal and pork, such as shoulder, don't really require browning. Likewise, chicken doesn't demand an advance sear, though you may prefer the look. However, other meats—beef and lamb, especially—truly benefit from this important step. The caramelization from browning enriches the accompanying sauce and eliminates the grayish appearance of meat put straight into the crock.

If you prefer the taste of browned meat but can't bring yourself to clean another pot or pan, one solution is to invest in a slow cooker with a built-in browning feature, such as the Breville Slow Cooker with Easy Sear technology, or the Crock-Pot Slow Cooker with Stovetop-Safe Cooking Pot, either of which allows you to brown and sauté right in the slow cooker itself—minus the added cleanup.

avoid ones in which the crock and heating unit are fused together, as that type of unit makes cleaning a particularly loathsome task.

Slow cookers with manual low and high settings work just fine, but for the ultimate set-and-forget experience, you'll want a slow cooker that's programmable. Unless you plan on coming home to turn off your slow cooker, a built-in timer can prevent your food from overcooking, and it might even automatically switch to a keep-warm function once the timer goes off after your meal is cooked. Even some slow cookers with manual settings have a keep-warm option, which is very nice to have when you want to serve warm food right from the bowl during parties.

These days, some slow cookers also come with a helpful searing function. This enables you to brown meat and sauté veggies directly in the unit. Spring for one with this feature if you can. You'll wash one less pan and benefit from the flavor the browning step gives, without any added hassle.

CUTS FOR THE CROCK

When it comes to choosing cuts of meat for the slow cooker, remember that everything is not created equal. Save lean, quick-cooking cuts like pork tenderloin for the stove top, oven, or grill. Opt, instead, for marbled, fatty, tougher cuts that benefit from a slow-and-low heat approach. This toughness is due to collagen, a fibrous connective tissue found in the muscles. Once broken down by the cooking process, moist and tender results await. As an added bonus, these preferred cuts are usually among the most affordable options in your grocery store and meat market.

BEEF

Look for fatty, marbled cuts, which provide the most flavor and cook until they're melt-in-your-mouth tender.

CUTS TO BUY: blade roast, brisket, chuck roast, oxtail, rump, shank, short ribs, shoulder

RECIPES TO TRY: Mexican Pot Roast (page 51) and Zesty Beef Brisket Sliders (page 62)

CUTS TO SKIP: lean, tender steaks, such as beef tenderloin

PORK

As with other meats, fatty, tough cuts of pork that require low and slow cooking are ideal.

CUTS TO BUY: pork shoulder (Boston butt or pork butt), rib roast, rump, shank

RECIPES TO TRY: Italian-Style Pork Shoulder (page 76) and Chinese Char Sui Ribs (page 92)

CUTS TO SKIP: thin-cut pork chops, pork tenderloin

FABULOUS FOIL

Want to make your slow cooker even more useful? Use a disposable slow cooker liner or line it with heavy-duty aluminum foil to eliminate the mess, reduce post-meal cleanup, and prevent food from sticking.

With casseroles and other layered dishes, create a foil "sling" by covering the inside of the crock with a crisscross of two or more pieces of foil, as needed. When your meal is ready, lift out the sling and cut your dish into individual portions.

To make sure your meat cooks evenly, take a tip from barbecue pitmasters and tightly wrap your protein in foil. This technique helps lock in moisture, tenderize meat, and speed the cooking process. Here's how: Place the meat on a large piece of foil, turn up the sides to form a bowl, and add ¼ cup of a liquid such as water, juice, beer, or wine. Tightly seal, then wrap with a second piece of foil and seal again to ensure no liquid (or steam) escapes. During cooking, the liquid will mix with the meat juices, effectively braising your meat or fish without drowning it in liquid from the slow cooker bowl. Check your food for doneness an hour or two sooner than the recipe requires since this technique tends to speed up the cooking process.

LAMB

Look for lamb cuts with fat running through them; they'll transform the humblest ingredients into something extraordinary.

CUTS TO BUY: middle neck, shank, and shoulder
RECIPES TO TRY: Tomato-Rosemary Braised Lamb Shanks with Chickpeas (page 105) and Lamb Shoulder with Smashed Root Vegetables (page 110)
CUTS TO SKIP: chops, fillet, leg

POULTRY

In the case of poultry, think dark meat. It yields juicier, richer results.

CUTS TO BUY: chicken or turkey thighs or drumsticks
RECIPES TO TRY: Chicken Cacciatore (page 122) and Chicken Tinga Tacos (page 139)
CUTS TO SKIP: lean white meat such as chicken or turkey breast

MAKING THE CASE FOR SEAFOOD

The cut and type of fish and seafood are not key to a successful slow cooker recipe. They all cook quickly. You may wonder, then, if there's any point to making fish recipes in your slow cooker. I absolutely think so. When they're prepared correctly, such dishes can be a unique and ultra-healthy take on the typical slow cooker meal. Plus, trapped beneath that slow cooker lid, that seafood scent won't permeate your home as strongly as it would if it were cooking in the oven.

There is, however, a compromise. Although you don't have to be chained to the slow cooker, fish and other seafood do need to be added toward the end of the cooking process to prevent overcooking, so you can't walk away entirely. For that reason, slow cooker seafood dishes aren't ideal for weekday meals if you won't be home to toss the fish in at the right time. Just save these recipes for the weekend or days off.

SPICE IT UP

An individualized combination of herbs and spices enhances each recipe in this book. If you're not entirely sure of the difference between herbs and spices, here's a brief definition: Herbs come from leafy plants, while spices come from dried seeds, fruit, bark, or the ground roots. Eliminate them, and your meal is bland.

SEASONING

Most dried herbs are ideal for the slow cooker, and they go in early right along with the other ingredients. Over time, they infuse cooking liquids with their concentrated flavor, and they are less expensive than fresh. A quick crush of your hand as you add dried herbs to a dish "wakes them up." Fresh herbs, on the other hand, do their best work—brightening and enlivening a dish—when added right before serving.

Beyond the flavors they impart, herbs and spices have been linked to health benefits, too. Basil has anti-inflammatory and antiviral properties. Capsaicin, the active ingredient in cayenne, helps boost circulation and aid in digestion. Oregano and marjoram, among other herbs, have long been used as health tonics.

STOCKING PANTRY ESSENTIALS

To make the full range of recipes in this book, you'll want to keep your kitchen stocked with these dried herbs and spices, most of which you likely already have.

ESSENTIAL HERBS

- Basil
- Bay leaves
- Chives
- Dill
- Marjoram
- Mint
- Oregano
- Rosemary
- Sage
- Thyme

GLOBAL FLAVORS

Authentic-tasting global cuisine can be created in your slow cooker with the right herb and spice blends. They add layers of distinct flavor to your home-cooked meal, while suggesting exotic locales. Here are a few blends I love:

CURRY POWDER If you thought curry powder came from India, think again. This British-born blend contains a widely varying combination of herbs and spices. Depending on the one you buy, it may include cumin, coriander, fenugreek, and turmeric, plus black cardamom, cinnamon, clove, coriander, cumin, garlic, ginger, green cardamom, mace, mustard seed, and red pepper.

CHINESE FIVE-SPICE POWDER There's little mystery here, as five spices make up this popular blend that goes with Chinese and non-Chinese dishes: cinnamon, cloves, fennel, star anise, and Szechuan peppercorns.

CHILI POWDER Closer to home, this indispensable ingredient in Southwestern and Tex-Mex cuisines typically features ground chiles along with cumin, garlic powder, oregano, and salt. It may also contain black pepper, cinnamon, cloves, coriander, mace, nutmeg, or turmeric.

From France's fines herbes to Ethiopian berbere, Jamaican jerk spice, or South Asia's garam masala, a well-stocked spice rack keeps your slow cooker meals anything but bland.

Classic Herb Pairings

- Beef + Thyme
- Pork + Sage
- Lamb + Rosemary
- Chicken + Thyme or Oregano
- Fish + Dill

ESSENTIAL SPICES

- Cayenne pepper
- Cinnamon
- Coriander
- Cumin
- Garlic powder
- Ginger
- Nutmeg
- Onion powder
- Paprika
- Red pepper flakes

Great Spice Pairings

- Chili + Cumin
- Spinach + Nutmeg
- Jambalaya + Cayenne
- Swedish meatballs + Allspice
- Teriyaki + Ginger

Keep dried herbs and spices in tightly closed containers stored in a cool, dark place away from heat and moisture. After about a year, they lose their punch and are best replaced.

TOP SLOW COOKER TIPS

By following a few basic steps, you'll enjoy a delicious, family-friendly meal straight out of the slow cooker. Just keep these seven easy tips in mind.

1. **BROWN AND SAUTÉ.** Some meats truly benefit from advance browning. By taking a little extra time to sauté vegetables and sear meat—beef and lamb, in particular—before adding them to the slow cooker, your dish will be layered with flavor.

2. **TRIM FAT.** When making a dish with rich gravy or sauce, be sure to trim any excess fat and/or remove the skin from the meat. Doing so prevents the liquid from becoming oily and greasy.

3. **ALCOHOL IN MODERATION.** In a slow cooker, alcohol doesn't have the chance to evaporate the way it would on the stove top in a pan without a lid. By all means, add a splash of wine or beer when a recipe calls for it, but there's no advantage to adding even more.

4. **USE THE RIGHT SETTING.** Slow cookers have a low and high setting. While the low setting (around 170°F) generally takes twice the cooking time of the high setting (often 280°F), some meats are better cooked more slowly than others.

5. **ADD DAIRY AT THE END OF COOKING.** Dairy products such as milk, cheese, sour cream, and yogurt should be added only during the final 15 minutes of cooking time. If added earlier they'll curdle or separate, effectively ruining your dish.

6. **TIGHTLY CLOSE AND DON'T OPEN THE LID.** It's tempting to peek. The problem is, slow cookers work by trapping heat and the resulting steam to create meltingly tender meat. So resist temptation, and only open the lid as needed or required.

7. **FINISH YOUR DISH WITH A SQUEEZE OR A SHOWER.** All dishes benefit from finishing touches—perhaps a squeeze of lemon or a shower of chopped fresh parsley. To maximize the effect, save this step until right before serving your meal.

RECIPES IN THIS BOOK

This cookbook aims to be your go-to for slow cooker recipes based around, or that go well with, meat. It offers a variety of classic dishes and soon-to-be favorites. All the recipes are intended for a 6-quart slow cooker. If you own a smaller appliance or are cooking only for one or two, the recipes can generally be cut in half. Otherwise, enjoy the leftovers! They almost always taste better the second day. And all the recipes *except for those that are dairy-based* can be frozen for future meals.

Some recipes include a browning or sautéing step for added flavor. While I've included this step if I think it really makes a difference, fundamentally it's optional. That's why the first numbered step of every recipe tells you what to add right into the slow cooker. The recipes don't depend on browning or sautéing first; I just happen to believe that those with the instructions to brown or sauté will come out better if you choose to do that step. In the end, it's up to you, your preferences, and the time you have.

A few recipes call for a final quick blitz in the blender for texture, but most require little to no pre-preparation. This means the ingredients go directly into one pot and there's nothing more to do until it's ready to eat. You may be asked to add an ingredient toward the end of cooking, such as the shrimp in Shrimp Creole (page 152), the sour cream in Pork Paprikash (page 82), or an optional zap of lemon-herb gremolata atop Osso Buco–Style Beef Shanks (page 71). These extra steps will only make the dish all the tastier.

ORGANIZATION

The recipe chapters are organized by type of protein (Beef, Pork, Lamb, Poultry, Seafood). You'll also find a chapter for broths and sauces, such as Chicken Stock (page 30) and Bordelaise Sauce (page 40), to give you a homemade option to include with the meat recipes; and another chapter for vegetables, sides, and dips like Smoky Baked Beans (page 168) and Hash Brown Casserole (page 163) to help make a complete meal.

FROM STOVE TOP TO SLOW COOKER

Do you have a favorite stove top- or oven-cooked dish that you wish you could prepare in the slow cooker instead? Odds are, you can, provided you follow a few rules of thumb.

- **Choose your meat wisely,** and swap it out as necessary because some cuts won't cook well in a slow cooker. Without compromising the integrity of your recipe, substitute a tougher, fattier, and more marbled cut for lean protein.

- If your original dish calls for **browning,** do so prior to simmering it in the slow cooker.

- **Flavors really concentrate** in the slow cooker, so you may need to reduce the amount of alcohol or potent spices used in a slow cooker version.

- **Liquid doesn't evaporate** from the slow cooker since the bowl remains covered throughout the whole cooking time. Generally speaking, liquid doesn't thicken either. To combat these tendencies, reduce the initial amount of braising liquid. However, bigger cuts such as pork shoulder may require a little additional liquid to kick-start the steam-cooking process. In such cases, adding a bit of extra liquid from the get-go helps break down the collagen in the meat more quickly.

- **Leaner, tougher cuts work best on the low setting** so they have enough time to become meltingly tender. Non-dairy-based soups and stews often work well cooked on a high setting, with the cooking time reduced.

- **To convert a recipe** from the stove top to the slow cooker, look to the original recipe. If a recipe cooks for an hour, it typically should cook no longer than six hours on the low setting. If the original recipe cooked for over an hour, it can usually cook on a slow cooker's setting for about 8 hours.

At the end of most recipes is a helpful tip such as a seasonal substitution, recommended wine pairing, suggestion for using leftovers, or advice on how to prep ingredients.

Everything is meant to be tasty and approachable. You won't need to invest in unusual or hard-to-find ingredients to make these dishes, nor will you need to labor over the slow cooker in order to cook a gourmet meal. You will, however, be proud to serve these meals to your family and company alike—not to mention devour them yourself.

CINNAMON APPLESAUCE (PAGE 47)

2

BROTH, STOCKS & SAUCES

WHETHER YOU'RE MAKING
soup that requires a rich stock, building layers of flavor for a meaty
entrée, or whipping up a sauce to accompany a roast, a good stock or
sauce can truly make or break the dish. This chapter is all about lay-
ing the groundwork for recipes to become something great. While
the terms *stock* and *broth* are often used interchangeably, stock is
made from bony parts and is richer than broth, which tends to be
made primarily from meat. If you're not making your own stock
from scratch, buy low-sodium store-bought stock, and season with
additional salt to taste.

4 pounds mixed
chicken bones

2 large onions

3 celery stalks, cut into
large chunks

8 garlic cloves, unpeeled

2 bay leaves

½ bunch parsley, stems
and leaves

1 teaspoon dried thyme

2 tablespoons peppercorns

1 teaspoon kosher salt,
plus more for seasoning

12 cups or more cold water,
enough to submerge meat
and vegetables

CHICKEN STOCK

Rich, hearty chicken stock is a real workhorse in the kitchen, serving as the basis for comforting soups, sauces, and long-simmered braises. For best results, roast the bones (along with the vegetables) before boiling them. Preheat your oven to 450°F and roast for 35 to 45 minutes, until golden brown. For an even richer broth, toss the bones and vegetables with 3 tablespoons olive oil and season with salt and pepper before roasting. Use this savory stock to flavor everything from Chicken Noodle Soup (page 125) to Barbecue Pulled Pork (page 77).

BOIL: Bring a large stockpot filled with water to a boil over high heat. Add the chicken bones and boil for 10 minutes. Drain the bones into a colander and rinse thoroughly with cold water.

1. Put the chicken bones into the slow cooker along with the onions, celery, garlic, bay leaves, parsley, thyme, peppercorns, salt, and water. Cover and cook on low for 8 hours.

2. Using a fine-mesh sieve or cheesecloth-lined colander, strain the broth and discard the solids. Season with additional salt, if needed. If using the stock right away, use a ladle or large spoon to skim and discard the fat that rises to the top. Otherwise, cover and store the stock in the refrigerator for up to 3 days and skim the solidified fat before using.

TIP: If you roast the bones, you may be tempted to skip boiling them, but I recommend both. To prevent scum from forming on the broth, boil the bones, then rinse them under cold water before making the stock. Any leftover parsley can be kept in the refrigerator for up to 2 weeks. First wash it in warm water, shake off the excess moisture, wrap in a dry paper towel, and seal in a plastic bag.

FISH STOCK

MAKES ABOUT
1 QUART

PREP
10 MINUTES

COOK
6 HOURS ON LOW

A delicious way to repurpose what would otherwise be thrown away, this seafood stock uses the scraps you have on hand after cooking fish or seafood. Use this recipe when making Seafood Stew (page 146) or Smoky Fish Soup with Vegetables (page 148) for extra-flavorful results.

1. Put the fish scraps into the slow cooker along with the salt, onion, fennel, celery, garlic, water, wine, parsley, bay leaves, and peppercorns. Stir to combine. Cover and cook on low for 6 hours.

2. Using a fine-mesh sieve or cheesecloth-lined colander, strain the stock and discard the solids. Season with additional salt, if needed, before using.

TIP: Store the stock in an airtight container in the refrigerator for up to 3 days or freeze for up to 3 months.

2 pounds fish scraps (bones, fish heads, seafood shells)

1 teaspoon kosher salt, plus more for seasoning

1 medium onion, chopped

1 large fennel bulb, trimmed and diced

1 celery stalk, chopped

2 garlic cloves, minced

4½ cups water

½ cup dry white wine

5 fresh parsley sprigs

2 bay leaves

½ teaspoon peppercorns

2 tablespoons olive oil

1½ pounds lamb shanks
(about 2 medium shanks)

3 bay leaves

3 medium garlic cloves

1 cup finely chopped onion

2 medium carrots,
finely chopped

1 medium parsnip,
finely chopped

2 celery stalks,
finely chopped

1 medium russet potato,
finely diced

8 cups Chicken Stock
(page 30) or low-sodium
if store-bought

1 teaspoon kosher salt,
plus more for seasoning

⅓ cup pearl barley

2 tablespoons finely
chopped fresh
parsley leaves

Freshly ground black pepper

SCOTCH BROTH

Scotch broth is a stick-to-your-ribs soup that originated in Scotland and is enjoyed the world over. The dish is typically made from stewing or braising cuts of lamb, mutton, or beef, with root vegetables and dried split peas or red lentils. In this version, I've used barley. Its tender, chewy texture is quite different than lentils or split peas, which essentially turn to mush. Leeks and cabbage are also common ingredients and can be added toward the end of cooking, in order to keep their texture. Use this recipe as a launching point to create your own variation.

BROWN: In a slow cooker with a stove-top function or in a Dutch oven or heavy-bottomed pan over medium-high heat, heat the oil until shimmering. Season the lamb shanks with salt and pepper, and brown, about 5 minutes per side.

1. Put the shanks in the slow cooker along with the bay leaves, garlic, onion, carrots, parsnip, celery, potato, stock, and salt. Cover and cook on low for 8 hours, until tender.

2. Using a ladle or large spoon, skim the fat during the final 45 minutes of cooking, and discard. At this point, transfer the shanks to a cutting board. When they are cool enough to handle, but still warm, tear the meat from the bones and discard the bones. Return the meat to the slow cooker and add the barley. The barley should be tender when done.

3. Season with additional salt and pepper, as needed. Stir in the parsley and serve.

TIP: This recipe is quite versatile. You can make it with other meats such as short ribs or beef shanks. If time allows, make Scotch Broth a day ahead but skip the fat-skimming. Chill the broth in the refrigerator. The next day, use a spoon to remove the layer of solid fat. Heat the broth, check the seasoning, finish with the parsley, and serve.

MAKES 12 CUPS

PREP
30 MINUTES

COOK
12 TO 18 HOURS
ON LOW

4 pounds mixed beef bones
(meaty marrow bones,
beef shanks, and bone-in
short ribs)

2 unpeeled carrots, cut into
large chunks

1 large yellow onion,
quartered

4 celery stalks, cut into
large chunks

1 head garlic, halved to
expose cloves

1 tablespoon peppercorns

1 teaspoon dried thyme

3 bay leaves

1¼ teaspoons kosher salt

12 cups or more cold water,
enough to submerge bones
and vegetables

BEEF BONE BROTH

Despite its deceptive name, the flavor of this "broth" is bolstered by bones. Therefore, it's technically a stock. To boost the broth's depth, roast the bones with fresh rosemary in an oven preheated to 450°F for 20 minutes before boiling them. You'll be rewarded with richer, meatier flavor overall.

BOIL: Bring a large stockpot filled with water to a boil over high heat. Add the beef bones and boil for 10 minutes. Drain the bones into a colander and rinse thoroughly with cold water.

1. Put the bones in the slow cooker along with the carrots, onion, celery, garlic, peppercorns, thyme, bay leaves, salt, and water. Cover and cook on low for 12 to 18 hours.

2. Using a fine-mesh sieve or cheesecloth-lined colander, strain the liquid and discard the solids. If using right away, use a ladle or large spoon to skim and discard the fat that rises to the top. Otherwise, cover the broth and store it in the refrigerator for up to 3 days. Use a spoon to remove the layer of solid fat before using.

TIP: Use this ultra-beefy broth as your base for sauces and stews such as Bordelaise Sauce (page 40) and Guinness Beef Stew (page 54), as well as for gravy. You can freeze the cooled broth in an airtight container for up to 6 months.

2½ pounds oxtail

1 onion

3-inch piece fresh
ginger, peeled

2 cinnamon sticks

2 teaspoons coriander seeds

1 teaspoon fennel seeds

5 whole star anise

5 whole cloves

1 whole cardamom pod

9 cups water

1½ tablespoons beef
base, such as Better
Than Bouillon

1½ tablespoons fish sauce

1 teaspoon sugar

1 teaspoon kosher salt

PHO STOCK

Healthy, hearty, rich, and fragrant all at once, Vietnamese pho is beloved and iconic for good reason. Roasting the bones before boiling them makes for a richer broth. Boiling bones prevents unwanted surface scum from muddling and clouding your broth. To make this stock into a soup, par-cook rice noodles and gather the add-ins, such as raw, ultra-thin slices of round steak, lime wedges, cilantro, Thai basil, mint, Thai chiles, bean sprouts, Sriracha, and hoisin sauce. When added into the hot broth, the noodles finish cooking and the meat cooks through.

BOIL: Bring a large stockpot filled with water to a boil over high heat. Add the oxtail and boil for 10 minutes. Drain the bones into a colander and rinse thoroughly with cold water.

1. Put the oxtail in the slow cooker along with the onion, ginger, cinnamon, coriander seeds, fennel seeds, star anise, cloves, cardamom, water, beef base, fish sauce, sugar, and salt. Cover and cook on low for 10 hours.

2. Using a fine-mesh sieve or cheesecloth-lined colander, strain the broth, and discard the spices and bones. Using a ladle or large spoon, skim and discard any scum or fat on the surface of the broth. Taste the broth and adjust the seasoning, if necessary.

TIP: I like to toast the spices on the stove top and char the onion and ginger before adding them to the slow cooker. Toast the spices in a frying pan over medium heat just until fragrant, taking care not to burn, about 30 seconds total. Char the onion and ginger in a preheated 450°F oven right along with the bones. After 10 minutes, turn the onion and ginger, then let them char for an additional 10 minutes before adding them to the slow cooker.

RICH MARINARA

SERVES 6

PREP
10 MINUTES

COOK
7 HOURS ON LOW

Marcella Hazan's tomato sauce is truly game changing. Made from the simplest of ingredients—canned tomatoes (I prefer the San Marzano variety), butter, and onion—it turns on end the idea of what a pasta sauce should be. Taking inspiration from her recipe, my version—which happens to be my son's favorite—is infused with the licorice-y flavor of basil, features garlic and a bit of heat, and gains depth from a splash of balsamic vinegar.

1. To the slow cooker, add the tomatoes, crushing them by hand, then add the butter, onion, basil, garlic, vinegar, salt, Italian seasoning, and red pepper flakes. Cover and cook on low for 7 hours.

2. Remove the cover and season with additional salt, if needed. Use an immersion blender or transfer to a blender to purée the sauce. Use the sauce immediately to top pasta, or cover and store in the refrigerator for up to 5 days.

TIP: Like Marcella Hazan, you may prefer to discard the onion before blending the sauce. I prefer to blend it along with the other tasty ingredients. The onion complements the tomatoes' acidity and the butter's nutty richness, and produces a more complex flavor.

2 (28-ounce) cans whole tomatoes

8 tablespoons unsalted butter

1 large onion, halved

3 large, fresh basil leaves

2 garlic cloves, smashed

1½ teaspoons balsamic vinegar

1½ teaspoons kosher salt, plus more for seasoning

1 teaspoon Italian seasoning blend

½ teaspoon red pepper flakes

SERVES 6

PREP
15 MINUTES

COOK
8 TO 10 HOURS
ON LOW

2 tablespoons extra-virgin olive oil

4 boneless beef short ribs

1¼ teaspoons kosher salt, plus more for seasoning

1½ pounds hot Italian sausage

1 large onion, finely chopped

1 celery stalk, finely chopped

1 large carrot, peeled and finely chopped

3 garlic cloves, minced

2 (28-ounce) cans crushed tomatoes

2 tablespoons tomato paste

2 teaspoons Italian seasoning

2 bay leaves

Freshly ground black pepper

½ cup grated Parmesan cheese, for garnish

MEATY ITALIAN GRAVY

While your *nonna* may have labored over a huge saucepan, diligently stirring a butcher counter's worth of meat to make Sunday gravy. The slow cooker—and a practical selection of protein—takes the work out of it, making it possible to enjoy hearty, tangy gravy on a weeknight.

BROWN: In a slow cooker with a stove-top function or in a Dutch oven or heavy-bottomed pan over medium-high heat, heat the oil until shimmering. Season the short ribs with salt and pepper, and brown, along with the Italian sausage, about 3 minutes per side.

1. Put the ribs and sausage in the slow cooker, along with the onion, celery, carrot, garlic, canned tomatoes, tomato paste, Italian seasoning, bay leaves, and salt. Stir to combine. Cover and cook on low for 8 to 10 hours.

2. Remove the lid and discard the bay leaves. Season with additional salt and pepper, if needed. Pour the sauce on pasta, toss, and serve immediately, passing the Parmesan at the table as a garnish.

TIP: The best Sunday-style gravy is made with a variety of cuts. Consider using a few additional meats, such as meatballs and diced pancetta, which add different flavors and textures. Feel free to incorporate your own favorites.

PEPPER STEAK SAUCE

MAKES 2 CUPS

PREP
10 MINUTES

COOK
6 HOURS ON LOW

Inspired by everyone's favorite steak sauce, A1, this version features red peppers for added sweetness and complexity. If you're into roast-y flavors, replace the fresh peppers with an equivalent number of fresh or jarred roasted red peppers.

1. To the slow cooker, add the peppers, garlic, ketchup, orange juice, tomato paste, mustard, vinegar, Worcestershire sauce, brown sugar, raisins, celery seed, salt, and pepper. Cover and cook on low for 6 hours.

2. About 1 hour before serving, transfer ¼ cup of sauce to a small bowl. Whisk in the flour until no lumps remain. Pour the mixture into the slow cooker, cover, and continue cooking until the sauce begins to thicken.

3. Season with additional salt and pepper, if needed. Use an immersion blender or transfer to a blender to purée the sauce. Use the sauce immediately, or cover and store in the refrigerator for up to 1 week.

TIP: Pair this sauce with a grilled steak, crisp salad, and a soft, medium-bodied red wine such as Pinot Noir.

3 large red peppers, seeded and roughly chopped

2 garlic cloves, smashed

¼ cup ketchup

¼ cup orange juice

2 tablespoons tomato paste

2 tablespoons Dijon mustard

2 tablespoons balsamic vinegar

2 tablespoons Worcestershire sauce

1 tablespoon brown sugar

1 tablespoon raisins

½ teaspoon celery seed

½ teaspoon kosher salt, plus more for seasoning

¼ teaspoon freshly ground black pepper, plus more for seasoning

3 tablespoons all-purpose flour

SERVES 4

PREP
15 MINUTES

COOK
8 TO 10 HOURS
ON LOW

1 tablespoon
unsalted butter

1 small onion, minced

2 garlic cloves, minced

5 tablespoons all-purpose
flour, divided

1½ pounds beef
marrow bones

1 cup Beef Bone Broth
(page 34) or low-sodium
if store bought

½ teaspoon kosher salt,
plus more for seasoning

¼ teaspoon freshly ground
black pepper, plus more
for seasoning

⅓ cup dry red wine,
such as Bordeaux

1 tablespoon
Worcestershire sauce

2 bay leaves

2 fresh thyme sprigs

BORDELAISE SAUCE

This lush French sauce, typically made in a pan, is a dynamite accompaniment to steak, especially buttery fillets. Because it's being made in the slow cooker, the sauce won't reduce the same way as it would if cooked on the stove top. If you prefer a thicker sauce, once it's strained, transfer the strained liquid to the same pan you cooked the steaks in. Deglaze the pan and reduce over medium-high heat for 5 minutes. Then add a pat of butter for extra glossiness before serving.

SAUTÉ: In a slow cooker with a stove-top function, or in a Dutch oven or heavy-bottomed pan on the stove over medium heat, melt the butter. Add the onion and garlic and sauté until translucent, stirring occasionally, about 10 minutes. Add 2 table-spoons of flour and stir to combine. Continue cooking for another 2 minutes to eliminate the raw taste of the flour.

1. Put the onion and garlic in the slow cooker, along with the marrow bones, broth, salt, pepper, wine, Worcestershire sauce, bay leaves, and thyme and cook on low for 8 to 10 hours.

2. About 1 hour before serving, transfer ¼ cup of sauce to a small bowl. Whisk the sauce with the remaining 3 tablespoons of flour until no lumps remain. (If the sauté step was omitted, whisk in the full 5 tablespoons of flour.) Pour the mixture back into the slow cooker. Cover and continue cooking until the sauce begins to thicken.

3. Using a fine-mesh sieve or cheesecloth-lined colander, strain the sauce and discard the solids. Season with additional salt and pepper, if needed. Use immediately or cover and store in the refrigerator for up to 3 days.

TIP: If you happen to have fresh parsley available, chop some up and use it to finish the dish. It'll lend a dash of visual brightness to this admittedly rich dish.

MAKES ENOUGH FOR
**3 POUNDS
OF WINGS**

PREP
5 MINUTES

COOK
6 HOURS ON LOW

1 (12-ounce) bottle
Louisiana-style hot sauce

½ cup (1 stick)
unsalted butter

2 tablespoons
Worcestershire sauce

2 teaspoons garlic powder

2 teaspoons onion powder

¼ teaspoon cayenne pepper

¼ teaspoon kosher salt,
plus more for seasoning

Freshly ground black pepper

BUFFALO WING SAUCE

Pretty much everyone loves wings, especially boneless wings. This easy and versatile sauce can also spice up a chicken sandwich. Just place some chicken breast on the bread of your choice, generously drizzle it with 2 tablespoons of the sauce, then top the entire sandwich with blue cheese dressing, and serve with a crunchy carrot-celery slaw on the side.

1. To the slow cooker, add the hot sauce, butter, Worcestershire sauce, garlic powder, onion powder, cayenne, and salt. Stir to combine. Cover and cook on low for 6 hours.

2. Season with additional salt and pepper, as needed.

TIP: To get crispy wings, first baste them with a generous amount of Buffalo wing sauce. Then deep-fry them in canola or peanut oil, or bake the wings on a well-greased baking tray in a preheated 425°F oven for 40 to 50 minutes, rotating the tray halfway through. (They do not need to be flipped.) Toss the wings with additional sauce before serving them piping hot.

ALFREDO SAUCE

I dare you to find someone who dislikes Alfredo sauce. Sure, there are some who indulge only occasionally given its richness, but the addictive flavor is hard to walk away from after that first taste. The most obvious use for this decadent sauce is over pasta, but also consider using it as well on a white pizza topped with roasted garlic and a mix of gooey Italian cheeses.

1. Use the cooking spray or olive oil to coat the inside (bottom and sides) of the slow cooker. Add the cream, chicken stock, butter, garlic, Parmesan, sherry, salt, and pepper and whisk to combine. Cover and cook on low for 4 to 6 hours.

2. About 30 minutes before serving, whisk in the flour. Leave the lid ajar and continue cooking until the sauce begins to thicken. Season with additional salt and pepper, if needed. Serve on pasta, passing additional Parmesan to sprinkle on top.

TIP: If you don't have dry sherry, you can substitute white wine, although the flavor won't be as robust. For a little color, add 1 cup of frozen peas right after whisking in the flour.

Cooking spray or
1 tablespoon extra-virgin olive oil

½ quart heavy
(whipping) cream

¼ cup Chicken Stock
(page 30) or low-sodium if store-bought

¼ cup butter, melted

2 garlic cloves, minced

1 cup finely shredded
Parmesan cheese, plus more for garnish

2 tablespoons dry sherry

¾ teaspoon kosher salt,
plus more for seasoning

½ teaspoon freshly ground
black pepper, plus more for seasoning

3 tablespoons
all-purpose flour

NACHO CHEESE SAUCE

SERVES 10

PREP
10 MINUTES

COOK
3 HOURS ON LOW

Serve this cheesy dip with corn tortilla chips, or use it to top nachos, along with chopped tomatoes, scallions, and black olives. If you like yours spicy, add a few dashes of Tabasco or additional red pepper flakes.

To the slow cooker, add the Velveeta and Cheddar, browned sausage, chiles, salt, pepper, chili powder, cumin, onion powder, garlic powder, oregano, and red pepper flakes. Cover and cook on low for 3 hours.

TIP: This cheesy dip can also be thinned out with chicken stock and turned into warming taco soup. It's a good way to use up the leftovers—if there *are* any leftovers—or make the soup from the get-go, in which case use about a quart of stock to start, and add more as needed.

1 (2-pound) box original Velveeta cheese, cut into chunks

8 ounces sharp Cheddar cheese, shredded

1 pound hot breakfast sausage, browned

1 (4-ounce) can chopped green or red chiles

1 teaspoon kosher salt

1 teaspoon freshly ground black pepper

1 tablespoon chili powder

1½ teaspoons ground cumin

½ teaspoon onion powder

¼ teaspoon garlic powder

¼ teaspoon dried oregano

¼ teaspoon red pepper flakes

2 cups ketchup

2 tablespoons tomato paste

1¼ cups water

¼ cup apple cider vinegar

1 tablespoon grainy mustard

1 teaspoon
Worcestershire sauce

3½ tablespoons packed
brown sugar

2 garlic cloves, minced

½ teaspoon red
pepper flakes

½ teaspoon kosher salt

½ teaspoon freshly ground
black pepper

1 bacon slice

1 bay leaf

BARBECUE SAUCE

Whether you intend to sauce some chops, slather on baby backs, or dunk some chicken tenders, this all-purpose barbecue sauce is the sort of thing you'll want to keep on hand. I also like to dip my fries in it or mix a touch of it into my slaw; it ups the flavor interest considerably.

1. To the slow cooker, add the ketchup, tomato paste, water, vinegar, mustard, Worcestershire sauce, brown sugar, garlic, red pepper flakes, salt, pepper, bacon, and bay leaf. Stir to combine. Cover and cook on low for 3 hours.

2. Remove and discard the bacon and bay leaf and let the sauce cool. Use immediately on chicken or ribs, or cover and refrigerate for up to 2 weeks.

TIP: Mix some of the leftover sauce into ranch dressing and drizzle it on a Southwestern-style Cobb salad loaded with sweet corn, cheddar, red onion, black beans, grilled chicken, and avocado. This sauce also tastes great with barbecue beef sandwiches. Just brown a pound of ground beef, stir in as much sauce as desired, and warm through in the pan or microwave before tucking into soft rolls.

CINNAMON APPLESAUCE

MAKES 6 CUPS

PREP
10 MINUTES

COOK
4 TO 6 HOURS ON LOW

Familiar and updated at once, this invitingly chunky applesauce is fragrant with cinnamon and brightened by lemon zest. Its sweet flavor is a perfect accompaniment to slow-roasted pork such as Italian-Style Pork Shoulder (page 76) or Ham with Root Vegetables (page 85).

4 pounds apples, mixed varieties, cored, peeled, and sliced

¼ cup white sugar

1½ tablespoons packed brown sugar

1 cinnamon stick

1 (2-inch) strip lemon peel

Pinch kosher salt

¼ cup water

1. To the slow cooker, add the apples, white sugar, brown sugar, cinnamon stick, lemon peel, salt, and water. Stir to combine. Cover and cook on low for 4 to 6 hours.

2. Remove and discard the cinnamon stick and lemon peel. Leave the sauce chunky, if desired, or mash with a fork until it reaches the desired consistency. Let the applesauce cool and serve immediately, or chill in an airtight container in the refrigerator for up to 2 weeks until ready to use.

TIP: You'll likely have leftovers—lucky for you. Enjoy the applesauce at breakfast the next morning, using it to top potato pancakes along with a dab of sour cream.

ZESTY BEEF BRISKET SLIDERS (PAGE 62)

3

BEEF

BEEF IS SO VERSATILE IT'S NO

wonder it's a prominent ingredient in meals no matter where you turn, making a focal appearance in everything from tacos to stir-fry to all-American cuisine. It's a beloved ingredient in soups and stews as well as sandwiches. Beef dishes are served on rice, in pasta, and often with potatoes whether they're of the sweet, savory, mashed, or fried variety. You can lighten up a beefy meal by serving a leafy green salad alongside your entrée. Nearly all of this chapter's recipes include a recommended browning step, as I think it truly improves the flavor of the finished dish. But feel free to experiment for yourself and decide whether you think it's necessary.

2 tablespoons olive oil

1 (4- to 5-pound) boneless chuck roast, trimmed of excess fat

4 medium onions, sliced

4 large carrots, peeled and cut into large chunks

4 medium waxy potatoes, such as Yukon Gold

2 cups Beef Bone Broth (page 34) or low-sodium if store-bought

½ cup red wine

1½ tablespoons Worcestershire sauce

3 bay leaves

¾ teaspoon kosher salt, plus more for seasoning

½ teaspoon freshly ground black pepper, plus more for seasoning

RED WINE POT ROAST

Meaty, tender, and aromatic, pot roast will bring your family to the table quickly. Make this recipe your own by adding other root vegetables, such as parsnips. You can also swap the wine for beer, or use sweet potatoes instead of the Yukon Golds. If you do, add the sweet potatoes an hour or two into the cooking time since they become tender more quickly.

BROWN: In a slow cooker with a stove-top function, or in a Dutch oven or heavy-bottomed pan over medium-high heat, heat the oil until shimmering. Season the roast with salt and pepper, and brown, about 3 minutes per side.

1. Put the meat in the slow cooker, along with the onions, carrots, potatoes, bone broth, wine, Worcestershire sauce, bay leaves, salt, and pepper. Cover and cook on low for 8 hours.

2. Using a ladle or large spoon, skim the fat from the cooking liquid. Remove and discard the bay leaves. Season with additional salt and pepper, as needed. Transfer the meat to a cutting board and let it rest for 10 minutes. Slice the meat and spoon some of the cooking liquid on top. Serve with the vegetables.

TIP: This is a versatile recipe, so I rarely make it the same way twice. Sometimes I add some grainy mustard and a few cherry bomb peppers. During the summer, I'll often grab a handful of herbs from the garden (thyme, basil, and oregano, for example), tie them together with kitchen twine, and throw them into the pot. They infuse the cooking liquid with flavor. Just be sure to discard them before serving.

MEXICAN POT ROAST

SERVES 6

PREP
15 MINUTES

COOK
8 TO 10 HOURS
ON LOW

Chili powder and jalapeños bring the heat to this pot roast. Ancho chili powder is commonly used in authentic Mexican cooking, but if you don't have any, another chili powder will work just fine. For the beer, choose a lager to add a clean, crisp flavor. This dish tastes great with mashed potatoes or Mexican rice. In my mind, though, it's not complete without a pot of smoky, soupy pinto beans and a pile of warm flour tortillas.

1. To the slow cooker, add the meat, onion, garlic, jalapeño, chipotle, tomatoes, bone broth, beer, Worcestershire sauce, vinegar, chili powder, cumin, bay leaves, and salt. Cover and cook on low for 8 to 10 hours.

2. Using a ladle or large spoon, skim the fat from the cooking liquid. Remove the bay leaves and discard. Season with additional salt, as needed. Serve immediately, or cover and store the roast in the refrigerator for up to 3 days.

TIP: Repurpose your leftovers as tacos, topping them with lime crema, made by mixing 1 cup of sour cream with 1 to 2 tablespoons lime juice. Or shred the meat and turn it into a Mexican-style chili with the pinto beans.

1 (3-pound) boneless bottom round roast

1 large onion, chopped

2 garlic cloves, minced

1 jalapeño pepper, finely chopped

1 canned chipotle chile en adobo, plus 1 tablespoon adobo sauce

1 (28-ounce) can crushed tomatoes

1 cup Beef Bone Broth (page 34) or low-sodium if store-bought

¼ cup beer

1 tablespoon Worcestershire sauce

1 tablespoon apple cider vinegar

1 tablespoon chili powder

1 tablespoon ground cumin

3 bay leaves

1 teaspoon kosher salt

SERVES 6

PREP
25 MINUTES

COOK
8 HOURS ON LOW

1½ tablespoons extra-virgin olive oil

1 (4-pound) boneless beef chuck roast

2 tablespoons tomato paste

1 cup dry red wine

¾ cup cider vinegar

1½ tablespoons white sugar

1 tablespoon pickling spices, wrapped in a sachet

4 carrots, chopped

1 large onion, chopped

1 cup Beef Bone Broth (page 34) or low-sodium if store-bought

8 gingersnap cookies, crushed

1 teaspoon kosher salt, plus more for seasoning

½ teaspoon freshly ground black pepper, plus more for seasoning

1½ tablespoons cornstarch

1½ tablespoons cold water

SAUERBRATEN

This comforting, yet boldly flavored, German pot roast has been linked to Charlemagne in the 9th century. The traditional (modern-day) version requires brining the meat in the refrigerator for several days. That step has been eliminated in favor of a quick stove-top preparation of the wine and vinegar, which gets added to the slow cooker with the meat. To make the pickling spice sachet, cut a 5-inch square of cheesecloth and place the pickling spice in the middle. Then gather up all four sides of the cloth and tie in the middle with kitchen twine.

BROWN: In a slow cooker with a stove-top function, or in a Dutch oven or heavy-bottomed pan over medium-high heat, heat the oil until shimmering. Season the roast with salt and pepper, and brown, about 3 minutes per side. Transfer the meat to a plate. Add the tomato paste and cook, stirring, for 1 minute. Whisk in the wine, vinegar, and sugar. Bring to a boil and simmer for 5 minutes.

1. If cooked outside the slow cooker, add the tomato-wine mixture to the slow cooker. Add the pickling spice sachet, carrots, onion, bone broth, gingersnaps, salt, and pepper. Stir to combine. Place the meat in the slow cooker. Cover and cook on low for 8 hours.

2. About 30 minutes before serving, remove the pickling spice sachet and discard. In a small bowl, whisk together the cornstarch and water. Add to the slow cooker and gently stir. Leave the lid slightly ajar and continue cooking until the liquid is thickened and the meat is tender. Using a ladle or large spoon, skim the fat from the top of the liquid and discard the spice packet. Season with additional salt and pepper, as needed, and add more sugar if the cooking juices taste too tart. Slice the meat and serve immediately with vegetables and gravy.

TIP: While sauerbraten is typically made with beef (rump or chuck roast), this dish can also be made with venison, pork, or lamb. Some regional versions add raisins toward the end of cooking to balance the acidity of this dish with the sweetness of the fruit.

2 tablespoons extra-virgin olive oil

3 pounds beef stew meat, cut into 1-inch chunks

2 tablespoons all-purpose flour

8 small waxy potatoes, such as Yukon Gold

4 large carrots, peeled and thinly sliced

2 medium parsnips, peeled and thinly sliced

2 large onions, thinly sliced

4 garlic cloves, thinly sliced

1 heaping tablespoon unsweetened cocoa

1 (15-ounce) can Guinness stout

1 cup Beef Bone Broth (page 34) or low-sodium if store-bought

1 tablespoon instant espresso powder

1 tablespoon Worcestershire sauce

¾ teaspoon kosher salt, plus more for seasoning

½ teaspoon black pepper, plus more for seasoning

¼ cup minced flat-leaf parsley, for garnish

GUINNESS BEEF STEW

While in the UK, I ordered this stew in a quintessential watering hole. I'll be honest: I wasn't impressed. It lacked the depth and nuance I expected. Chalk it up to bad luck! To rectify that, this version employs a combination of unsweetened cocoa, espresso powder, and Worcestershire sauce. These ingredients complement the chocolate-y flavor of the stout.

BROWN: In a slow cooker with a stove-top function, or in a Dutch oven or heavy-bottomed pan over medium-high heat, heat the oil until shimmering. Season the meat with salt and pepper. In a large bowl, toss the meat with the flour and brown, about 3 minutes per side.

1. Put the meat in the slow cooker, along with the potatoes, carrots, parsnips, onions, garlic, cocoa, and stout. If you skipped browning, in a small bowl, whisk the flour into the bone broth until no lumps remain. Add it to the slow cooker with the espresso, Worcestershire sauce, salt, and pepper. Stir to combine. Cover and cook on low for 8 hours.

2. Using a ladle or large spoon, skim the fat from the surface. Season with salt and pepper, as needed. Ladle into bowls and garnish with the parsley.

TIP: If you have fresh herbs on hand, by all means, use them. Toss some bay leaves in the cooking liquid along with a few sprigs of fresh thyme. Elevate the dish further by serving it with some horseradish cream, which is a quickly made mix of sour cream, grated fresh horse-radish, salt, and pepper.

KOREAN BEEF STEW

SERVES 6

PREP
15 MINUTES

COOK
8 HOURS ON LOW

I adore spicy food, so odds are my slow cooker version sports more of a kick than you're used to. If you prefer a bit less, feel free to cut back on the chili paste. Kimchi can be found in most well-stocked grocery stores, usually in the refrigerated section by the fresh wontons, pea pods, and other chilled Asian ingredients.

BROWN: In a slow cooker with a stove-top function, or in a Dutch oven or heavy-bottomed pan over medium-high heat, heat the oil until shimmering. Season the beef with salt and pepper, and brown, about 3 minutes per side.

1. Put the beef in the slow cooker, along with the onion, garlic, water, soy sauce, rice wine, kimchi, sesame oil, chili paste, salt, and pepper. Cover and cook on low for 8 hours.

2. Season with additional salt and pepper, as needed. Serve immediately, or cover and store in the refrigerator for up to 3 days.

TIP: Consider pairing this spicy dish with a crisp, cold beer. If I can get my hands on it, Asahi Super Dry cools the tongue especially well. A bowl of fluffy white rice can be served alongside to tame the flames, too.

2 tablespoons vegetable oil

3 pounds beef stew meat, cut into 1-inch pieces

1 medium onion, finely chopped

2 garlic cloves, minced

2 cups water

2 tablespoons soy sauce

2 tablespoons rice wine

½ cup cabbage kimchi, chopped

1½ tablespoons sesame oil

1 tablespoon gochujang chili paste or Sriracha

¾ teaspoon kosher salt, plus more for seasoning

½ teaspoon freshly ground black pepper, plus more for seasoning

SERVES 8

PREP
15 MINUTES

COOK
8 HOURS ON LOW

2 tablespoons vegetable oil

1 (4-pound) boneless chuck roast, trimmed of excess fat

1 small onion, finely chopped

5 garlic cloves, minced

3 canned chipotle chiles en adobo, plus 2 tablespoons sauce

3 cups Beef Bone Broth (page 34) or low-sodium if store-bought

2 tablespoons apple cider vinegar

1 tablespoon chili powder, preferably ancho

2 teaspoons ground cumin

1½ teaspoons dried oregano

½ teaspoon ground allspice

3 bay leaves

1 teaspoon kosher salt, plus more for seasoning

½ teaspoon freshly ground black pepper

Chopped red onion, for garnish

Chopped cilantro, for garnish

Salsa, for garnish

Lime wedges, for garnish

BARBACOA

Taqueria-style beef barbacoa—or "authentic tacos" as my 12-year-old calls them—is one of my favorite meals. Generously seasoned and slow-braised until the beef is fall-apart tender, barbacoa may become one of yours, too. Chuck roast is my preferred cut for this recipe, but short ribs or brisket also work. Serve it in warm corn tortillas and top with chopped red onions, cilantro, salsa, and a squeeze of fresh lime juice.

BROWN: In a slow cooker with a stove-top function, or in a Dutch oven or heavy-bottomed pan over medium-high heat, heat the oil until shimmering. Season the chuck roast with salt and pepper, and brown, about 3 minutes per side.

1. Put the meat in the slow cooker, along with the onion, garlic, chiles, bone broth, vinegar, chili powder, cumin, oregano, allspice, bay leaves, salt and pepper. Cover and cook on low for 8 hours.

2. Discard the bay leaves. Using two forks, shred the meat inside the slow cooker. Discard any fatty bits. Season with additional salt, as needed. Serve with corn tortillas and bowls of red onion, cilantro, salsa, and limes.

TIP: The shredded beef can be stored in an airtight container in the refrigerator for up to 3 days, or frozen for 6 months. Leftover tacos are always amazingly good, but when you want to switch things up, use any remaining barbacoa with your favorite taco pie recipe later in the week.

CLASSIC BEEF AND BEAN CHILI

SERVES 6

PREP
15 MINUTES

COOK
8 HOURS ON LOW

Chili is a perfect meal for a large group because it can be customized with toppings of your guests' choosing. My family enjoys their chili with a choice of lime wedges, chopped red onions, minced jalapeños, grated Cheddar, sour cream, and elbow macaroni noodles. And—not just for kids—a handful of corn chips for crunch.

BROWN: In a slow cooker with a stove-top function, or in a Dutch oven or heavy-bottomed pan over medium-high heat, heat the oil until shimmering. Add the ground beef and brown, breaking it up into small bits. When almost no pink remains, add the bell pepper, celery, onion, and garlic, and continue cooking, stirring occasionally, until the vegetables start to soften, about 7 minutes.

1. If browned outside the slow cooker, place the beef and vegetables in the slow cooker now. Add the kidney beans, tomatoes, tomato paste, chili powder, cumin, cocoa, salt, and bay leaves, and stir to combine. Cover and cook on low for 8 hours.

2. Discard the bay leaves. Season with additional salt, as needed. Serve immediately or cover and refrigerate for up to 3 days.

TIP: If you're feeling ambitious, turn your leftover chili into chili pie. Follow the directions of your favorite cornbread recipe to make the batter. Mix in a handful of grated cheese, spread the batter on top of the chili, and cook in the oven as directed. Top the chili pie with a dollop of sour cream and a dash of taco sauce or salsa before serving.

2 tablespoons extra-virgin olive oil

2 pounds ground beef

1 red bell pepper, seeded and finely diced

1 celery stalk, finely chopped

1 large onion, finely chopped

4 garlic cloves, minced

2 (15-ounce) cans kidney beans, drained and rinsed

1 (28-ounce) can crushed tomatoes

1 (6-ounce) can tomato paste

¼ cup chili powder

1 tablespoon ground cumin

2 teaspoons unsweetened cocoa

1½ teaspoons kosher salt, plus more for seasoning

2 bay leaves

SERVES 4

PREP
10 MINUTES

COOK
8 HOURS ON LOW

1 pound ground beef,
at least 25% fat

1 pound ground pork

1 large onion, minced,
divided

8 garlic cloves,
minced, divided

¼ cup grated
Parmesan cheese

¼ cup dry bread crumbs

1 large egg

½ cup minced
flat-leaf parsley

1½ teaspoons kosher
salt, divided, plus more
for seasoning

1 teaspoon freshly ground
black pepper, divided

3 (28-ounce) cans
crushed tomatoes

½ teaspoon red
pepper flakes

1 teaspoon Italian seasoning

ITALIAN MEATBALLS

The proper meatball preparation is a hotly contested topic. Everyone, it seems, has an opinion on the matter. Sometimes I brown my meatballs in a pan before plunking them into the sauce to finish cooking. I might broil them instead. Other times, as with this recipe, I do not brown them at all, opting instead to poach the meatballs in the sauce. This approach infuses the sauce with rich, meaty flavor, while helping keep the meatballs tender. Serve them atop your favorite pasta and pass the Parmesan.

1. In a large bowl, combine the beef and pork with half the onion, half the garlic, the Parmesan, bread crumbs, egg, parsley, ½ teaspoon of salt and ½ teaspoon of pepper. With your hands, gently combine the ingredients, taking care not to overwork the meat. Form the meat mixture into golf ball–size balls. Refrigerate them until ready to use.

2. Put the tomatoes, red pepper flakes, Italian seasoning, the remaining 1 teaspoon of salt, and remaining ½ teaspoon of black pepper into the slow cooker. Stir to combine. Cover and cook on low for 8 hours.

3. About 45 minutes before serving, gently add the meatballs to the sauce. Season with additional salt, as needed. Cover and finish cooking. Serve immediately.

TIP: To further improve the flavor of the sauce, place a sprig of fresh basil and a few sprigs of fresh thyme into the slow cooker before starting. Be sure to discard the herbs before serving.

SERVES 6

PREP
15 MINUTES

COOK
6 HOURS ON LOW

1 pound ground beef,
at least 25% fat

1 pound ground pork

1 small onion, minced

2 garlic cloves, minced

¼ cup dry bread crumbs

1 large egg

1 teaspoon kosher salt,
divided, plus more
for seasoning

½ teaspoon freshly ground
black pepper, divided, plus
more for seasoning

⅛ teaspoon ground allspice

⅛ teaspoon ground nutmeg

2 cups Beef Bone Broth
(page 34) or low-sodium
if store-bought

½ cup heavy
(whipping) cream

2 tablespoons
all-purpose flour

1 teaspoon
Worcestershire sauce

½ teaspoon red wine vinegar

1 bay leaf

¼ cup finely chopped
flat-leaf parsley

SWEDISH MEATBALLS

Unlike other types of dairy, heavy cream won't curdle during cooking. It will thicken a bit, however, resulting in a lush, silky sauce—just the thing for these Swedish meatballs. This dish is traditionally served with lingonberry jam alongside boiled baby potatoes, but I also like them on a bed of egg noodles.

1. In a large bowl, combine the beef and pork with the onion, garlic, bread crumbs, egg, ½ teaspoon of salt, ¼ teaspoon of pepper, the allspice, and nutmeg. Use your hands to gently combine the ingredients, taking care not to overwork the meat. Using 1 tablespoon-size portions, form the meat into balls. Refrigerate until ready to use.

2. In the slow cooker, whisk together the bone broth, cream, flour, Worcestershire sauce, vinegar, bay leaf, remaining ½ teaspoon of salt and remaining ¼ teaspoon of pepper until no lumps remain. Cover and cook on low for 6 hours.

3. About 30 minutes before serving, carefully add the meatballs into the sauce. Cover and finish cooking. Discard the bay leaf. Season with additional salt and pepper, as needed. Serve, garnished with the parsley.

TIP: It's important to add the meatballs toward the end of the cooking time so they don't end up dry and overcooked. Adding them during the last half-hour infuses the sauce with meaty flavor, and that's another plus.

CORNED BEEF AND CABBAGE

SERVES 8

PREP
10 MINUTES

COOK
8 HOURS ON LOW

There are probably as many variations of this traditional St. Patrick's Day fare as there are cooks who make it. I didn't grow up a fan of corned beef and cabbage, but I've come around in my adulthood, namely because I serve it with a horseradish condiment that adds a little more bite. To make it, just mix ¼ cup of drained horseradish, ¼ cup of grainy mustard, and 1 cup of sour cream.

1. Put the meat in the slow cooker, along with the pickling spice, carrots, onion, garlic, and potatoes. Pour the water and beer on top. Cover and cook on low for 8 hours.

2. About 1 hour before serving, add the cabbage to the slow cooker. Cover and continue to cook. When the meat and vegetables are done, discard the cooking liquid. To serve, thinly slice the meat against the grain and serve with the vegetables. Be sure to pass the butter for melting on top of the cabbage.

TIP: There are two main cuts of beef brisket: point-cut and flat-cut. I recommend the flat-cut because it will result in meat that's more easily sliced. Point-cut is more likely to turn into shreds when you attempt to slice it.

1 (4 pound) flat-cut corned beef brisket, trimmed of excess fat

2 tablespoons pickling spice

4 large carrots, peeled and cut into large chunks

1 large onion, thinly sliced

2 garlic cloves, thinly sliced

10 small red potatoes, halved

4 cups water

6 ounces beer

1 small head green cabbage, cored and roughly chopped

2 tablespoons unsalted butter

MAKES
12 SLIDERS

PREP
10 MINUTES

COOK
8 TO 10 HOURS
ON LOW

1½ tablespoons extra-virgin olive oil

1 (3-pound) flat-cut beef brisket, trimmed of excess fat

2 pounds small potatoes, scrubbed and left whole

3 carrots, peeled and cut into chunks

1 medium onion, minced

2 (14.5-ounce) cans fire-roasted, diced tomatoes

1 tablespoon brown sugar

¼ cup dry red wine

1½ tablespoons balsamic vinegar

1 tablespoon Worcestershire sauce

1 teaspoon kosher salt

½ teaspoon freshly ground black pepper

12 soft slider rolls, sliced

1 large red onion, sliced

ZESTY BEEF BRISKET SLIDERS

Brisket Sliders are like a grown-up version of Sloppy Joes, but they're a little more sophisticated in taste and less likely to end up on your shirt. This version melds a vinegary tang with a touch of brown sugar, resulting in a deeply flavorful sauce that's perfect for piling onto soft rolls.

BROWN: In a slow cooker with a stove-top function, or in a Dutch oven or heavy-bottomed pan over medium-high heat, heat the oil until shimmering. Season the brisket with salt and pepper, and brown, about 4 minutes per side.

1. Put the brisket in the slow cooker, along with the potatoes, carrots, onion, tomatoes, brown sugar, wine, vinegar, Worcester-shire sauce, salt, and pepper. Stir to combine. Cover and cook on low for 8 to 10 hours, or until tender. Remove the cover, taste, and adjust the seasonings, as needed.

2. Transfer the brisket to a cutting board and let it rest for 10 minutes. Slice the meat against the grain. Remove the vegetables from the slow cooker and reserve them for another use.

3. Divide the meat evenly into 12 servings and tuck the brisket into each roll. Spoon the sauce on top of the sliders. and add 1 or 2 slices of red onion per slider.

TIP: A boon for busy cooks, brisket is even better when cooked, refrigerated, and sliced for serving the next day. Store it in an airtight container, unsliced, in the refrigerator. Then, rewarm it before cutting it to serve.

FRENCH DIP

There's something awfully satisfying about plunking a meaty sandwich into a bowl of salty, savory jus. Here, the slow cooker works its magic to turn out tender, savory-sweet braised beef, meant to be tucked into French rolls that get dipped—hence the recipe's name—in a mouthwatering broth.

BROWN: In a slow cooker with a stove-top function, or in a Dutch oven or heavy-bottomed pan over medium-high heat, heat the oil until shimmering. Season the roast with salt and pepper, and brown, about 3 minutes per side.

1. Put the meat in the slow cooker, along with the onion, garlic, bone broth, Coca-Cola, Worcestershire sauce, onion powder, oregano, salt, pepper, and bay leaves. Cover and cook on low for 6 hours.

2. Using a ladle or large spoon, skim the fat from the top of the liquid and discard the bay leaves. Season with additional salt and pepper, as needed. Transfer the roast to a cutting board and let it rest for 10 minutes. Divide the meat to make six servings, then slice and tuck the meat into the French rolls. Serve with a bowl of the braising jus for dipping.

TIP: If you're home while this is cooking, your best bet is to remove and slice the meat at the 3- or 4-hour mark. Return the slices to the cooking jus. Doing so will prevent the meat from falling apart while being sliced later. If you're not around and need to cook the meat for the 6 hours straight through, no worries—it'll taste great that way, too.

SERVES 6

PREP
15 MINUTES

COOK
6 HOURS ON LOW

1 tablespoon extra-virgin olive oil

1 (3-pound) boneless chuck roast, timed of excess fat

1 medium onion, finely chopped

6 garlic cloves, very thinly sliced

2 cups Beef Bone Broth (page 34) or low-sodium if store-bought

1 cup Coca-Cola Classic

3 tablespoons Worcestershire sauce

½ teaspoon onion powder

½ teaspoon dried oregano

½ teaspoon kosher salt, plus more for seasoning

½ teaspoon freshly ground black pepper, plus more for seasoning

2 bay leaves

6 French rolls, for serving

SERVES 6

PREP
25 MINUTES

COOK
8 HOURS ON LOW

1 tablespoon extra-virgin
olive oil

3 pounds beef stew meat

3 thick-cut bacon slices,
finely chopped

3 tablespoons
all-purpose flour

1 cup fruity red wine

2 tablespoons cognac
or brandy

1 pound fresh
mushrooms, sliced

3 carrots, peeled and sliced
on the bias

18 pearl onions, peeled

2 garlic cloves, smashed

2 cups Beef Bone Broth
(page 34) or low-sodium
if store-bought

2 bay leaves

¾ teaspoon kosher salt,
plus more for seasoning

½ teaspoon freshly ground
black pepper, plus more
for seasoning

1½ tablespoons cornstarch

1½ tablespoons cold water

BEEF BOURGUIGNON

This French dish takes a bit more effort to prepare than some, but it's a vastly simplified version of what's fully prepared in a Dutch oven. Because mushrooms tend to get rubbery in the slow cooker, they're best placed beneath the meat. Line the slow cooker with them, and let the heat "roast" them, while the cooking liquid gives them a gentle braise. A Burgundy or Beaujolais wine works best in this dish.

BROWN: In a slow cooker with a stove-top function, or in a Dutch oven or heavy-bottomed pan over medium-high heat, heat the oil until shimmering. In a large bowl, gently toss the beef and bacon with salt, pepper, and the flour, and brown, about 4 minutes per side. Add the wine and cognac, then raise the heat to high and deglaze the pan, scraping the brown bits from the bottom.

1. If browned, transfer the meat and bacon to a plate. Line the bottom of the slow cooker with the mushrooms. Place the meat and bacon on top of the mushrooms. Add the carrots, pearl onions, and garlic.

2. If you skipped browning, whisk the flour into the bone broth until no lumps remain. Add it to the slow cooker with the bay leaves, salt, and pepper. Cover and cook on low for 8 hours.

3. About 30 minutes before serving, whisk together the cornstarch and water in a small bowl. Add to the slow cooker and gently stir. Leave the lid slightly ajar and continue cooking until the cooking liquid has thickened and the meat is tender. Discard the bay leaves. Using a ladle or large spoon, skim the fat from the top of the liquid or refrigerate for a couple of hours until the fat solidifies and can be spooned off. Season with additional salt and pepper, as needed.

TIP: Fresh herbs really enliven this dish. Chop ½ cup of fresh flat-leaf parsley and garnish your stew with it right before serving. It's also nice to have something to sop up the tasty juices; thinly sliced, toasted garlic bread does the trick.

SERVES 8

PREP
10 MINUTES

COOK
6 TO 8 HOURS ON LOW

1½ tablespoons extra-virgin olive oil

1 (3- to 4-pound) boneless chuck roast

1¼ teaspoons kosher salt

1½ teaspoons freshly ground black pepper

¼ cup all-purpose flour

4 tablespoons (½ stick) unsalted butter

10 pepperoncini

2 tablespoons mayonnaise

1 tablespoon sour cream

2 teaspoons apple cider vinegar

1 teaspoon buttermilk

½ teaspoon dried dill

½ teaspoon dried chives

MISSISSIPPI BEEF ROAST

Credited to Mississippi resident Robin Chapman, who shared her recipe on "Good Morning America" in 2016, this dish went on to become a viral sensation on Pinterest and among mom bloggers. Originally made with one packet each of dry ranch seasoning and au jus (see tip), this adaptation continues the unexpectedly flavorful theme. Serve this main course atop noodles, rice, or mashed potatoes. A simple green salad nicely completes this meal.

BROWN: In a slow cooker with a stove-top function, or in a Dutch oven or heavy-bottomed pan over medium-high heat, heat the oil until shimmering. Season the roast with the specified amount of salt and pepper, and coat with the flour. Brown the roast on both sides to create a crust, about 4 minutes per side.

1. Place the roast in the slow cooker, along with the butter, pepperoncini, mayonnaise, sour cream, cider vinegar, buttermilk, dill, and chives. Cover and cook on low for 6 to 8 hours, until tender.

2. Transfer the meat to a cutting board. Using two forks, shred the meat and discard any fat. Return the meat to the slow cooker and mix the meat with the liquid inside, or plate the meat and drizzle the tangy au jus on top.

TIP: If you don't want to trouble yourself with homemade ranch ingredients, eliminate the mayonnaise, sour cream, and buttermilk from the recipe. Replace them with one packet of dry ranch seasoning, one packet of dry au jus seasoning, and ¼ cup of water.

CHICAGO-STYLE ITALIAN BEEF

SERVES 6

PREP
15 MINUTES

COOK
4 HOURS ON LOW

Deli meat? It's what brings the taste of authenticity to Italian Beef. I like to use deli meat from the Vienna or Scala's brands for this dish. An eye of round cut tastes good, too, but it won't resemble the real thing when made entirely in the slow cooker, as it falls apart in shreds. My favorite version of this dish incorporates hot Italian sausage to create a quintessential combo sandwich: au jus–dunked Chicago original stuffed with both meats, topped with peppers, and served with hot giardiniera. Fortunately, you don't have to live in Chicago to find a jar of these pickled vegetables; you'll find it in most supermarkets.

1. In the slow cooker, place the deli meat, onions, bell peppers, garlic, paprika, salt, cayenne, oregano, pepper, bone broth, wine, and Worcestershire sauce. Stir to combine. Cover and cook on low for 4 hours.

2. Slice the French bread and, for each sandwich, tuck some Italian Beef between two pieces of bread. Top with some of the cooking liquid and a few pieces of bell pepper. Serve with the giardiniera.

TIP: If you prefer an eye of round to deli meat, try roasting it yourself, with the fat intact, in the oven prior to adding it to the slow cooker. This will help prevent it from falling apart. Then thinly slice it and proceed with the recipe.

3 pounds thinly sliced deli-style Italian beef

2 large onions, thinly sliced

2 red bell peppers, seeded and sliced

6 garlic cloves, very thinly sliced

1 tablespoon smoked sweet paprika or Hungarian paprika

1 teaspoon kosher salt

1 teaspoon cayenne pepper

1 teaspoon dried oregano

½ teaspoon freshly ground black pepper

1½ cups Beef Bone Broth (page 34) or low-sodium if store-bought

1 cup dry red wine

3 tablespoons Worcestershire sauce

Loaf of French bread, for the sandwich

Jar of hot giardiniera, for garnish

PAPRIKA-SPIKED BEEF AND SWEET POTATO STEW

SERVES 6

PREP
15 MINUTES

COOK
8 TO 10 HOURS
ON LOW

Hearty, smoky, and russet-hued beef and sweet potato stew is just the thing to take the nip out of a cold winter evening. It's perfectly satisfying as is, though I also recommend serving it with egg noodles, 16 ounces for 6 people.

BROWN: In a slow cooker with a stove-top function, or in a Dutch oven or heavy-bottomed pan over medium-high heat, heat the oil until shimmering. Season the meat liberally with salt and pepper and brown on all sides until caramelized, about 5 minutes.

1. Put the beef in the slow cooker, along with the paprika, caraway, onion, garlic, bell pepper, sweet potatoes, chicken broth, vinegar, Worcestershire sauce, tomato paste, and bay leaves and stir to combine. Cover and cook on low for 8 to 10 hours, until the meat and vegetables are tender.

2. Remove the cover and discard the bay leaves. Season with additional salt and pepper, as needed. Sprinkle the pepitas on top of individual portions before serving.

TIP: This stew can—and arguably should—be prepared a day before and placed in the refrigerator to allow the flavors to deepen. Reheat the next day and enjoy.

1 to 1½ tablespoons extra-virgin olive oil

1 (3-pound) boneless beef stew meat

¾ teaspoon kosher salt, plus more for seasoning

¼ teaspoon freshly ground black pepper, plus more for seasoning

1 tablespoon paprika

¼ teaspoon ground caraway seed

1 large onion, chopped

2 garlic cloves, minced

1 small red bell pepper, seeded and finely chopped

2 medium sweet potatoes, peeled and cut into large chunks

1 cup Chicken Broth (page 30) or low-sodium if store-bought

3 tablespoons red wine vinegar

1 tablespoon Worcestershire sauce

¼ cup tomato paste

2 bay leaves

¼ cup pepitas, lightly toasted

SERVES 6

PREP
20 MINUTES

COOK
8 HOURS ON LOW

1½ tablespoons extra-virgin olive oil

1 (3-pound) boneless beef chuck roast

½ teaspoon kosher salt, plus more for seasoning

½ teaspoon freshly ground black pepper, plus more for seasoning

1 medium onion, finely chopped

3 garlic cloves, minced

1½ cups Beef Bone Broth (page 34) or low-sodium if store-bought

1 tablespoon Worcestershire sauce

1 tablespoon grainy mustard

1 teaspoon red wine vinegar

½ cup beer

2 bay leaves

1½ tablespoons all-purpose flour

½ cup sour cream

2 teaspoons chopped fresh dill, or ½ teaspoon dried dill

1 package egg noodles, cooked

BEEF STROGANOFF

This popular dish originates in Russia. Featuring near-endless variations, some featuring paprika, others made with chicken, this iteration is hardly definitive. However, it sure does taste good. I suggest serving it with a Russian cucumber salad (see Tip); its acidity is a nice counterpart to the creamy richness of the sauce.

BROWN: In a slow cooker with a stove-top function, or in a Dutch oven or heavy-bottomed pan over medium-high heat, heat the oil until shimmering. Season the roast with the salt and pepper. Brown the roast, about 3 minutes per side.

1. Put the chuck roast in the slow cooker, along with the onion, garlic, beef broth, Worcestershire sauce, mustard, vinegar, beer, and bay leaves. Cover and cook on low for 8 hours.

2. Using a ladle or large spoon, skim the fat from the top of the liquid and discard the bay leaves. Transfer the liquid to a medium saucepan over medium-high heat. Whisk in the flour until no lumps remain. Add the sour cream and dill and whisk to combine. Simmer for 3 to 4 minutes to allow the sauce to thicken. Season with salt and pepper, as needed.

3. Using two forks, shred the meat. Top the noodles with the meat and spoon the sauce on top. Serve immediately.

TIP: To make Russian cucumber salad, slice very thinly 2 medium cucumbers, 6 radishes, and 2 green onions. Add them to a salad bowl along with ½ cup sour cream, 1½ teaspoons white vinegar, and 2 tablespoons freshly chopped dill. Stir to combine and season with salt and pepper.

OSSO BUCO-STYLE BEEF SHANKS

SERVES 4

PREP
15 MINUTES

COOK
6 HOURS ON LOW

Osso buco is traditionally made with veal, which can be very expensive. In the slow cooker, beef shanks work even better. My favorite way to finish this Italian dish is with a generous sprinkle of gremolata, a chopped herb relish made from parsley, lemon zest, and garlic. It cuts through the richness of the meat, and it looks really pretty, too.

BROWN: In a slow cooker with a stove-top function, or in a Dutch oven or heavy-bottomed pan on the stove over medium-high heat, heat the oil until shimmering. On a large plate or cutting board, lightly spread the flour. Season the shanks with salt and pepper and dredge them in the flour. Brown the meat, about 3 minutes per side.

1. Put the shanks in the slow cooker, along with the onion, celery, tomato paste, garlic, wine, bone broth, vinegar, Italian seasoning, bay leaves, salt, and pepper. Cover and cook on low for 6 hours.

2. Discard the bay leaves and rosemary. Using a ladle or large spoon, skim the fat from the top of the braising liquid. Season with additional salt and pepper, as needed. Arrange the shanks on a platter or plate individually and serve.

TIP: Because liquid doesn't evaporate from the slow cooker, the sauce will be rather thin. If you prefer a thicker sauce, use a fine-mesh sieve or cheesecloth-lined colander to strain the braising liquid into a medium saucepan. Whisk in 2 tablespoons of flour until no lumps remain, and bring to a rolling boil on the stove top. Continue whisking until it reaches a gravy-like thickness. Then, serve with the shanks.

1½ tablespoons extra-virgin olive oil

6 cross-cut, bone-in beef shanks

½ cup all-purpose flour

1 medium onion, diced

1 celery stalk, diced

2½ tablespoons tomato paste

4 garlic cloves, minced

½ cup dry white wine

1 cup Beef Bone Broth (page 34) or low-sodium if store-bought

1½ teaspoons balsamic vinegar

½ teaspoon Italian seasoning

2 bay leaves

1 fresh rosemary sprig

¾ teaspoon kosher salt, plus more for seasoning

½ teaspoon freshly ground black pepper, plus more for seasoning

12 leaves Savoy cabbage

1 to 1½ tablespoons
extra-virgin olive oil

1 pound ground beef

¼ cup finely chopped onion

2 garlic cloves, minced

1 cup cooked rice

1 large egg, beaten

1 teaspoon kosher salt,
plus more for seasoning

½ teaspoon freshly ground
black pepper, plus more
for seasoning

2 cups tomato sauce

1 tablespoon brown sugar

1 tablespoon apple
cider vinegar

1 teaspoon
Worcestershire sauce

STUFFED CABBAGE ROLLS

Beef and rice–stuffed cabbage rolls manage to be both simple and impressive at the same time. (And also satisfying and tasty.) The Worcestershire-spiked tomato sauce creates an appetizing contrast to the pale green parcels of cabbage, and a tangy counterpart to the meat and rice inside. The sauce gets its sweet tang from a touch of apple cider vinegar and brown sugar. Remember to spoon more of it on the rolls before serving. The cabbage leaves need to be boiled before going into the slow cooker, otherwise their leaves won't be pliable enough to form the rolls. The beef browning step here is not optional—the meat must be cooked before being added to the rolls.

1. Set a large pot with 8 cups water on the stove and heat until boiling, about 15 minutes. Submerge the cabbage leaves in the boiling water for 3 minutes. Drain and reserve.

2. In a slow cooker with a stove-top function, or in a Dutch oven or heavy-bottomed pan on the stove over medium-high heat, heat the oil until shimmering. Brown the ground beef, breaking it into small chunks, until almost no pink remains. Add the onion and garlic and continue cooking until the vegetables soften, about 4 minutes.

3. Transfer the cooked mixture to a large bowl. Add the rice, egg, salt, and pepper and stir to combine.

4. In a medium bowl, mix together the tomato sauce, brown sugar, vinegar, and Worcestershire sauce.

5. On a large work surface such as a butcher block or counter top, place 2 or 3 of the cabbage leaves at a time. Place about ¼ cup of the meat mixture in the center of each leaf. Gently fold in the sides of the leaf and roll into parcels, like you would a burrito.

6. Place the cabbage rolls in the slow cooker. Pour the tomato sauce mixture over the cabbage rolls. Cover and cook on low for 8 hours.

7. Season with additional salt and pepper, as needed. Serve the cabbage rolls, spooning the sauce on top.

TIP: If you have fresh thyme, it's a welcome addition to this hearty meal. Toss in three sprigs and let them infuse the sauce with flavor. Discard the sprigs before serving.

BRAZILIAN PORK FEIJOADA (PAGE 99)

4

PORK

PORK IS A STAR IN A VARIETY

of dishes and cuisines. Whether it's pulled and turned into tacos, stuffed into sausage, smothered in creamy or tangy sauces, or roasted low and slow until it practically melts in your mouth, pork has certainly earned its rightful place on our tables. Plus, it goes with most everything, whether it's a roast paired with Cinnamon Applesauce (page 47) or barbecued with a side of Cheesy Creamed Corn with Bacon (page 160). Add that to the fact that it works wonderfully well across a wide range of cuisines, making it a mainstay among global cooking enthusiasts.

SERVES 8

PREP
15 MINUTES

COOK
10 TO 12 HOURS
ON LOW

6 garlic cloves, smashed

1 teaspoon ground fennel

1 teaspoon ground coriander

½ teaspoon freshly ground
black pepper

1½ teaspoons kosher salt

1½ tablespoons extra-virgin
olive oil

1 tablespoon freshly
squeezed lemon juice

1 (5½-pound) whole bone-in
pork shoulder

ITALIAN-STYLE PORK SHOULDER

Tender pork shoulder is a Sunday supper superstar, though this recipe is easy enough to make any day of the week. That said, its crust of garlicky fennel, black pepper, and coriander elevates this dish above ordinary fare. Make it the centerpiece of a meal with a side of buttery vegetables along with roasted potatoes, pasta, or crusty sourdough bread.

1. In a small bowl, combine the garlic, fennel, coriander, pepper, and salt. Using a fork, mash them into a chunky paste. Add the oil and lemon juice and continue mashing until all the ingredients are well combined. Liberally slather the mixture on the pork shoulder, and place the meat in the bowl of the slow cooker. Cover and cook on low for 10 to 12 hours.

2. Transfer the pork to a cutting board and let it rest for 15 minutes. With a ladle or large spoon, skim the fat from the pan juices. When cool enough to handle, use two forks to shred the meat or use your fingers to pull the meat off the bone in rustic chunks, discarding the fat. Place the meat on a platter, drizzle with the liquid from the slow cooker, and serve.

TIP: Perfect for a large dinner party, this hefty roast can be paired with a bottle of crisp, dry Sauvignon Blanc or Pinot Grigio.

BARBECUE PULLED PORK

SERVES 8

PREP
10 MINUTES

COOK
10 HOURS ON LOW

Barbecue is the ultimate flavor-packed choice during the summer for feeding a slew of people with very little effort. Even better, Barbecue Pulled Pork can be made year-round in your slow cooker. If you're anything like me, you appreciate a little crunch on your sandwich. I top mine with coleslaw and salty potato chips (even salt-and-vinegar flavored, if I plan ahead).

1 (4-pound) pork shoulder

1 large onion, chopped

3 garlic cloves, minced

2 cups Barbecue Sauce (page 46) or store-bought

¾ cup Chicken Stock (page 30) or low-sodium if store-bought

½ teaspoon ground coriander

½ teaspoon kosher salt

½ teaspoon freshly ground black pepper

6 ounces beer

1 tablespoon packed dark brown sugar

8 soft hamburger buns or Kaiser rolls, sliced

1. Put the pork shoulder in the slow cooker and add the onion, garlic, barbecue sauce, chicken stock, coriander, salt, pepper, beer, and brown sugar. Stir to combine and spoon over the pork shoulder. Cover and cook on low for 10 hours.

2. Transfer the pork to a cutting board. If the pork has a bone, remove it with a sharp knife and discard the bone. Use two forks to shred the meat, discarding any undesirable bits of fat. Return the meat to the slow cooker and stir to coat with the sauce.

3. Divide the meat evenly into 8 servings and serve on the buns.

TIP: If you prefer your barbecue lightly sauced, place the shredded meat in a large bowl instead of returning it to the slow cooker. Add the sauce a spoonful at a time until you reach your desired level of sauciness.

2 canned chipotle chiles
en adobo, minced, plus
1 tablespoon adobo sauce

1 (28-ounce) can
puréed tomatoes

1 large onion, finely chopped

4 garlic cloves, minced

1½ tablespoons chili
powder, preferably ancho

1 tablespoon ground cumin

2 teaspoons dried oregano

2 teaspoons ground paprika

½ teaspoon
ground cinnamon

½ teaspoon kosher salt

½ teaspoon freshly ground
black pepper

2 teaspoons apple
cider vinegar

1 (4-pound) boneless
pork shoulder

2 teaspoons coarse cornmeal

½ cup chopped fresh
cilantro, for garnish

PORK CHILI CON CARNE

This hearty, no-bean chili is about as stick-to-your-ribs as you can get. Its fragrance comes from smoky chipotles and deeply flavorful ground ancho chile, along with aromatic cumin, cinnamon, paprika, and oregano. (Use Mexican oregano for this recipe if you can.) If you have some unsweetened cocoa lying around, I wouldn't discourage you from adding 1½ teaspoons of that, too.

1. Put the chipotle chiles, adobo sauce, tomatoes, onion, garlic, chili powder, cumin, oregano, paprika, cinnamon, salt, pepper, and vinegar in the slow cooker and stir to combine. Place the pork shoulder in the slow cooker and spoon the sauce on top. Cover and cook on low for 10 hours.

2. About 30 minutes before serving, transfer the pork to a cutting board. Stir the cornmeal into the chili, cover with the lid, and continue cooking. Using two forks, shred the meat, discarding any undesirable bits of fat. Return the meat to the slow cooker and stir it into the sauce. Ladle the chili into bowls and garnish with the cilantro.

TIP: For the most nuanced chili, de-seed, toast, grind, and reconstitute a mix of 3 New Mexico, 2 árbol, and 3 ancho chiles. Then, purée and add them to the mixture instead of the dried, ground ancho chili powder the recipe calls for.

PORK AND BEANS

SERVES 8

PREP
10 MINUTES

COOK
12 HOURS ON LOW

This childhood classic gets a fresh face in a slow cooker version that incorporates smoky elements (bacon, barbecue sauce) and tang from ketchup and vinegar. Molasses and brown sugar are added to balance the flavors. I don't recommend using pork chops or loin in this recipe due to the long cooking time, which all but guarantees that such cuts will dry out.

1. In the slow cooker, add the tomato purée, ketchup, barbecue sauce, chicken stock, molasses, onion, bacon, vinegar, brown sugar, garlic powder, mustard powder, salt, pepper, and beans. Stir to combine. Season the pork with additional salt and pepper, and place in the slow cooker on top of the beans. Cover and cook on low for 12 hours, or until the meat is fork-tender and the beans are tender when pierced with a fork.

2. Transfer the pork to a cutting board and shred the meat, discarding any undesirable fatty bits. Transfer the shredded meat back to the slow cooker and mix it with the beans. Season with additional salt and pepper, as needed, and serve.

TIP: If you're in a hurry, try cooking this dish on high for 5 to 6 hours. Remember, though, that the cooking time varies with this dish, as it is highly dependent on the variety and age of the beans (older beans take longer to become tender). During cooking, you may need to add additional cooking liquid, such as stock, as the beans will absorb a great deal.

1 cup canned tomato purée

1 cup ketchup

½ cup Barbecue Sauce (page 46) or store-bought

½ cup Chicken Stock (page 30) or low-sodium if store-bought

1 tablespoon molasses

1 large onion, finely chopped

3 bacon slices, finely chopped

2 tablespoons white vinegar

2 tablespoons packed brown sugar

1 teaspoon garlic powder

1 teaspoon mustard powder

1 teaspoon kosher salt, plus more for seasoning

½ teaspoon freshly ground black pepper, plus more for seasoning

3½ cups raw dry navy beans, picked over, soaked overnight, drained and rinsed

1 (3-pound) boneless pork shoulder

1 tablespoon extra-virgin olive oil

6 (1-inch-thick) blade, shoulder, or sirloin pork chops

4 large, unpeeled Idaho Yukon Gold potatoes, scrubbed clean and cut into long wedges

5 garlic cloves, minced

1 tablespoon dried oregano

3 slices lemon

1 teaspoon kosher salt, plus more for seasoning

½ teaspoon freshly ground black pepper, plus more for seasoning

½ cup dry white wine

½ cup Chicken Stock (page 30) or low-sodium if store-bought

PORK CHOPS
WITH POTATOES

I'm a proud Chicagoan and, like any self-respecting resident, I love its signature dishes, including punchy Chicken Vesuvio. When done right, it's truly a treat because the skin gets all crackly in the oven. This adaptation sports the same flavors, but it uses thick-cut pork chops instead of chicken. Because pork chops are lean, this isn't a dish you should leave in the slow cooker all day. Save it for when you can manage the shorter cooking time. For added color and authenticity, add 1 cup of frozen peas during the last 20 minutes of cooking time. Cover and continue cooking until they're steamed through.

BROWN: In a slow cooker with a stove-top function, or in a Dutch oven or heavy-bottomed pan over medium-high heat, heat the oil until shimmering. Season the pork chops with salt and pepper, and brown, about 3 minutes per side.

1. If browned, transfer the pork chops to a plate. Line the bottom of the slow cooker with the potatoes and place the pork chops on top. Add the garlic, oregano, lemon slices, salt, pepper, wine, and chicken stock. Cover and cook on low for 4 to 6 hours.

2. Discard the lemon slices. Taste and season with additional salt and pepper, as needed. Serve immediately, spooning the cooking liquid on top of the meat and potatoes.

TIP: Pair this dish with a crisp Italian white wine, such as Pinot Grigio from the cool Collio wine region near Venice.

3 pounds pork stew meat

1 large onion, finely chopped

1 large red or yellow bell pepper, seeded and chopped

2 garlic cloves, minced

1 cup Chicken Stock (page 30) or low-sodium if store-bought

3 tablespoons red wine vinegar

1 tablespoon Worcestershire sauce

¼ cup tomato paste

1 tablespoon paprika

½ teaspoon kosher salt, plus more for seasoning

½ teaspoon freshly ground black pepper, plus more for seasoning

¼ teaspoon ground caraway

½ cup sour cream

1 pound egg noodles, cooked

PORK PAPRIKASH

This Hungarian stew is commonly made with chicken and owes its name to the generous amount of paprika that flavors the rich, creamy sauce. It's important to wait until the end of cooking to add the sour cream or else you'll encounter unpleasant, curdled results.

1. To the slow cooker, add the pork, onion, bell pepper, garlic, chicken stock, vinegar, Worcestershire sauce, tomato paste, paprika, salt, pepper, and caraway. Stir to combine. Cover and cook on low for 6 hours.

2. About 20 minutes before the end of the cooking time, season with additional salt and pepper, as desired. Add the sour cream and stir to combine. Continue cooking until the ingredients are warmed through. Serve on top of the egg noodles.

TIP: Make this Hungarian stew more authentic by seasoning the meat with salt and pepper and then browning it in bacon fat before proceeding with the rest of the recipe.

SAUSAGE JAMBALAYA

SERVES 8

PREP
10 MINUTES

COOK
8 HOURS ON LOW

There's no need to wait until Mardi Gras to enjoy this spicy New Orleans dish. Feel free to customize it to your taste. For example, consider adding some boneless, skinless chicken thighs at the start, followed by peeled, deveined shrimp at the same time you add the cooked rice—shortly before serving.

1. To the slow cooker, add the sausage, celery, onion, bell pepper, garlic, jalapeño, cayenne, Cajun seasoning, bay leaves, thyme, chicken stock, and tomatoes. Cover and cook on low for 8 hours.

2. About 25 minutes before serving, taste and season with additional Cajun seasoning, as needed. Discard the bay leaves and thyme sprigs. Stir in the rice. Cover and continue cooking until warmed through. Spoon the jambalaya into bowls and serve.

TIP: Rice cooked in the slow cooker turns mushy. Instead, prepare a pot of rice on the stove top and stir it in shortly before serving so it retains its bite.

1½ pounds smoked pork sausage, such as andouille, sliced

3 celery stalks, finely chopped

1 large onion, finely chopped

1 large red bell pepper, seeded and finely chopped

4 garlic cloves, minced

1 jalapeño pepper, finely chopped

1 teaspoon cayenne pepper

1 tablespoon Cajun seasoning

2 bay leaves

3 fresh thyme sprigs or ½ teaspoon dried thyme

4 cups Chicken Stock (page 30) or low-sodium if store-bought

1 (28-ounce) can diced tomatoes (preferably fire-roasted), undrained

4 to 5 cups cooked long-grain white rice

Cooking spray or
1 tablespoon extra-virgin
olive oil

3 pounds waxy,
unpeeled potatoes,
such as Yukon Gold, cut
into ¼-inch-thick disks

1½ cups shredded sharp
Cheddar cheese

1 medium onion,
finely chopped

2 garlic cloves, minced

1½ cups diced cooked ham

½ teaspoon garlic powder

½ teaspoon kosher salt,
plus more for seasoning

½ teaspoon freshly ground
black pepper, plus more
for seasoning

½ cup heavy
(whipping) cream

1 cup Chicken Stock
(page 30) or low-sodium
if store-bought

HAM AND SCALLOPED POTATOES

I love scalloped potatoes, whether they're served as a side or as a main course. They're even delicious for breakfast. As if these weren't reasons enough to make them, they're also a great way to use up that leftover Ham with Root Vegetables (page 85).

1. Use the cooking spray or olive oil to coat the inside (bottom and sides) of the slow cooker. Add the potatoes, cheese, onion, garlic, ham, garlic powder, salt, and pepper and stir to combine. Pour the heavy cream and chicken stock on top. Cover and cook on low for 6 to 8 hours.

2. Season with additional salt and pepper, as needed, and gently stir before serving.

TIP: It's important to use waxy potatoes, which is why I've recommended Yukon Golds. Idaho potatoes just don't hold up—they become mealy in the slow cooker. Also, note that I've opted to leave the potatoes unpeeled. This is because the skin helps hold the potatoes together while they cook. Otherwise, you end up with mush.

HAM WITH ROOT VEGETABLES

SERVES 10

PREP
10 MINUTES

COOK
4 TO 6 HOURS ON LOW

Special enough for the holidays but simple enough for every day of the week, this ham tastes extra savory thanks to the addition of balsamic vinegar, Dijon mustard, and tangerine juice. If you can't get your hands on tangerine juice, orange juice is a fine substitute.

1. Use the cooking spray or olive oil to coat the inside (bottom and sides) of the slow cooker. Score the ham fat all over with a diamond pattern, about ¼-inch deep, using a sharp knife. Spread about half of the brown sugar in the bottom of the slow cooker and place the ham on top, scored-side down. Scatter the carrots, parsnips, and turnips around the ham.

2. In a medium bowl, whisk together the remaining ½ cup or so of the remaining brown sugar, the Dijon, vinegar, tangerine juice, butter, garlic, sage, pepper, and salt. Pour over the ham and vegetables, taking care to rub the mixture into the crevices of the ham. Cover and cook on low for 4 to 6 hours.

3. Transfer the ham to a cutting board and let it rest for 10 minutes. Use a fine-mesh sieve or cheesecloth-lined colander to strain the cooking liquid into a serving bowl, and discard the solids. Slice the ham, arrange on a serving platter, and drizzle with the juices. Serve immediately.

TIP: This recipe feeds a crowd, though any leftovers make for great sandwiches. Pan-fry a few slices in the morning and use the meat to fill a toasted English muffin, along with a slice of melty cheese, and a yolky (over-easy) fried egg. Save the ham bone to make a soup such as Split Pea Soup with Ham (page 88).

Cooking spray or 1 tablespoon extra-virgin olive oil

1 (5- to 6-pound) bone-in ham

1¼ cups packed brown sugar, divided

4 carrots, peeled and cut into large chunks

4 parsnips, peeled and cut into large chunks

2 turnips, peeled and cut into large chunks

½ cup Dijon mustard

¼ cup balsamic vinegar

¼ cup freshly squeezed tangerine or orange juice

3 tablespoons butter, melted

3 garlic cloves, thinly sliced

½ teaspoon dried sage

½ teaspoon freshly ground black pepper

½ teaspoon kosher salt

PORK CARNITAS

SERVES 6

PREP
5 MINUTES

COOK
3 HOURS ON HIGH

Rick Bayless is the inspiration behind these easy, ultra-flavorful carnitas, which sizzle atop a bed of pork lard, resulting in tender meat and crispy nubs that are reminiscent of those served at taquerias. If you can't get pork lard from a Mexican grocery store (far better tasting than grocery-store-Crisco) or prefer not to use lard at all, steep the seasoned meat on low in a mixture of seasoned, canned, fire-roasted tomatoes, garlic, and serranos. Serve up your carnitas on warm corn tortillas, topped with ranchero-style beans, chopped red onion, minced cilantro, diced avocado, salsa, and a squeeze of fresh lime juice.

1 cup fresh pork lard

1 teaspoon kosher salt

1 teaspoon dried oregano, preferably Mexican

1 teaspoon chili powder, preferably ancho

1 (3- to 4-pound) boneless pork shoulder, cut into 1-inch cubes

1. Place the lard in the slow cooker and turn to high. Rub the salt, oregano, and chili powder into the pork. When the lard has melted, place the pork in a single layer on top of the lard. Cover and cook on high until tender, about 3 hours.

2. Transfer the meat to a cutting board, leaving the fat in the slow cooker. Use two forks to roughly shred the meat into large chunks. Tuck the carnitas into warm corn tortillas and add your favorite toppings.

TIP: Souping up a pot of canned ranchero-style beans on the stove top is a cinch. Just brown two slices of finely diced bacon in a medium saucepan until crispy. Remove the bacon and drain on paper towels. Discard all but 1 tablespoon of bacon fat. Add 1 medium chopped onion, one finely diced serrano pepper, and 1 minced garlic clove and sauté over medium heat until softened, about 5 minutes. Add 1 (15-ounce) can of diced, fire-roasted tomatoes. Season with salt and pepper, as needed, and simmer on low for 20 minutes, stirring occasionally.

SERVES 6

PREP
10 MINUTES

COOK
6 TO 8 HOURS ON LOW

SPLIT PEA SOUP
WITH HAM

2 pounds dried green split peas, picked over and rinsed

1 celery stalk, chopped

1 large carrot, peeled and chopped

1 small onion, chopped

2 fresh thyme sprigs or ¼ teaspoon dried thyme

½ teaspoon seasoned salt, plus more for seasoning

¼ teaspoon freshly ground black pepper, plus more for seasoning

1 bay leaf

1 leftover ham bone (see Ham with Root Vegetables, page 85)

6 cups water

Anderson's pea soup is a quaint California tradition, one my partner, Mike, introduced me to during an epic road trip along the Pacific Coast Highway. We pulled off the road, and I skeptically obliged, thinking it was going to be geriatric-friendly, non-California-type roadside fare. And then I tried it—and understood. This hearty soup is inspired by that delicious bowl and amazing trip.

1. To the slow cooker, add the split peas, celery, carrot, onion, thyme, seasoned salt, pepper, bay leaf, ham bone, and water and stir to combine. Cover and cook on low for 6 to 8 hours.

2. Discard the ham bone and bay leaf. Purée using an immersion blender or transfer to a blender to purée until smooth. Season with additional seasoned salt and pepper, as desired. Ladle into bowls and serve.

TIP: I've added a ham bone for smokiness, though you can certainly leave it out. The original Anderson's split pea soup is vegetarian—vegan, in fact.

LASAGNA SOUP

SERVES 6

PREP
15 MINUTES

COOK
8 HOURS ON LOW

I've certainly come across recipes for slow cooker lasagna, but I can't recommend them. Pasta cooked for too long tastes off to me. As a compromise, this Italian sausage–spiked soup contains the same flavors as in its traditional form, from its tomato base to its ricotta topping, but the quick-cooking pasta is added shortly before serving so it doesn't turn to mush.

BROWN: In a slow cooker with a stove-top function, or in a Dutch oven or heavy-bottomed pan over medium-high heat, heat the oil until shimmering. Brown the Italian sausage, breaking it up into small bits until no pink remains.

1. Put the Italian sausage in the slow cooker, along with the onion, garlic, chicken stock, tomatoes, wine, Italian seasoning, salt, pepper, and red pepper flakes. Cover and cook on low for 8 hours.

2. During the final hour of cooking, add the macaroni. Cover and continue cooking until tender.

3. In a small bowl, combine the ricotta and Parmesan. Season with salt and pepper and stir to combine. Season the soup with additional salt and pepper, as needed. Ladle the soup into bowls and top with a dollop of the ricotta mixture before serving.

TIP: Brighten the dish with minced herbs such as basil and parsley. A zap of lemon zest makes a stellar addition, too.

1 tablespoon extra-virgin olive oil

¾ pound hot or sweet Italian pork sausage, casings removed

1 medium onion, finely chopped

3 garlic cloves, minced

6 cups Chicken Stock (page 30) or low-sodium if store-bought

1 (28-ounce) can puréed tomatoes

¾ cup dry red wine

2 teaspoons dry Italian seasoning

½ teaspoon kosher salt, plus more for seasoning

½ teaspoon freshly ground black pepper, plus more for seasoning

¼ teaspoon red pepper flakes

8 ounces dried elbow macaroni or ditalini

½ cup ricotta cheese, plus more for garnish

½ cup shredded Parmesan cheese

6 large baking potatoes

1 large onion, finely chopped

3 garlic cloves, minced

2 bacon slices, uncooked, plus 6 slices cooked and crumbled, divided

1¼ teaspoons kosher salt, plus more for seasoning

1 teaspoon freshly ground black pepper, plus more for seasoning

1 quart Chicken Stock (page 30) or low-sodium if store-bought

1 cup heavy (whipping) cream

½ cup sour cream, for garnish

1 cup shredded sharp Cheddar cheese, for garnish

2 scallions, thinly sliced, for garnish

SMOKY BAKED POTATO SOUP

Loaded baked potatoes—in soup form, no less—is the kind of meal pretty much everyone can get behind. Here, uncooked bacon slices flavor the soup. They are discarded before the soup is served and replaced with crispy crumbles, along with all the anticipated toppings.

1. To the slow cooker, add the potatoes, onion, garlic, 2 slices of uncooked bacon, the salt, pepper, and chicken stock. Stir to combine. Cover and cook on low for 8 hours.

2. Discard the bacon slices and stir in the heavy cream. Season with additional salt and pepper, as needed. Continue cooking until warmed through. Ladle the soup into bowls and garnish with the sour cream, Cheddar, scallions, and cooked, crumbled bacon.

TIP: If you have fresh chives growing in the garden, they make a welcome addition. Chop some up and use them in place of, or in addition to, the sliced scallions.

BALSAMIC PORK ROAST

SERVES 6

PREP
10 MINUTES

COOK
6 TO 8 HOURS ON LOW

The balsamic tang of this pork roast is offset by a touch of honey and brown sugar. If you're going to use pork loin for this dish, make sure you ask your butcher to leave the fat cap on. This will prevent the meat from drying out while cooking. Otherwise, swap the roast out for a fattier cut such as pork shoulder.

BROWN: In a slow cooker with a stove-top function, or in a Dutch oven or heavy-bottomed pan over medium-high heat, heat the oil until shimmering. Season the pork loin with salt and pepper, and brown, about 3 minutes per side.

1. Place the pork roast, fat-side up in the slow cooker. In a small bowl, whisk together the garlic, chicken stock, vinegar, mustard, brown sugar, Worcestershire sauce, honey, salt, and pepper. Pour over the roast. Cover and cook on low for 6 to 8 hours.

2. Transfer the roast to a cutting board, and let it rest for 10 minutes. Meanwhile, use a ladle or large spoon to skim the fat from the sauce. Thinly slice the pork roast, transfer to a platter, and drizzle with the cooking juices. Serve immediately.

TIP: Pork is so versatile that you have near-endless options when it comes to sides. Serve it with oven-roasted potatoes or sweet potatoes when it's cold outside. Come summer, throw together a salad of grilled, shaved-from-the-cob sweet corn, zucchini, and peppers.

1½ tablespoons extra-virgin olive oil

1 (3- to 4-pound) boneless pork loin

2 garlic cloves, minced

1 cup Chicken Stock (page 30) or low-sodium if store-bought

½ cup balsamic vinegar

2 tablespoons Dijon mustard

1 tablespoon brown sugar

1 tablespoon Worcestershire sauce

½ tablespoon honey

½ teaspoon kosher salt

½ teaspoon freshly ground black pepper

Cooking spray or
1 tablespoon extra-virgin
olive oil

2 racks of St. Louis–
style spareribs, cut into
individual ribs

½ cup hoisin sauce

½ cup soy sauce

¼ cup Chicken Stock
(page 30) or low-sodium
if store-bought

2 tablespoons rice wine

2 tablespoons brown sugar

3 garlic cloves, minced

½ teaspoon Chinese
five-spice powder

CHINESE CHAR SUI RIBS

Sweet, salty, and sticky, these Asian ribs lend themselves to slow cooking. To my taste, though, they're best when they've been caramelized— it's a benchmark of this popular dish, in fact. So, I strongly suggest a brief trip to the broiler before serving these beauties. A bowl of white rice makes the perfect accompaniment.

1. Use the cooking spray or olive oil to coat the inside (bottom and sides) of the slow cooker. Place the ribs in the slow cooker. In a small bowl, whisk together the hoisin sauce, soy sauce, chicken stock, rice wine, brown sugar, garlic, and five-spice powder until combined. Pour the mixture over the ribs. Cover and cook on low for 8 hours.

2. Preheat the broiler. Transfer the ribs to an aluminum foil–lined baking sheet. Baste the ribs with the cooking sauce. Broil until the ribs have caramelized and charred in spots, 3 to 5 minutes. Serve immediately with the remaining sauce.

TIP: If you want that vibrant red hue of your favorite Chinese restaurant version, add a few drops of red food coloring to your char sui sauce.

6 (1-inch-thick) blade, shoulder, or sirloin pork chops

1 medium onion, sliced

2 garlic cloves, minced

½ cup soy sauce

1½ teaspoons Chinese black vinegar or white vinegar

¼ cup packed brown sugar

½ teaspoon ground ginger

¼ teaspoon Chinese five-spice powder

2 cups snap peas

CHINESE-STYLE PORK CHOPS

Packed with flavor, these Asian pork chops are a worthy alternative to takeout, and can be prepped in less time than it takes to place an order. Be sure to use thick-cut chops so they stay moist and don't overcook. Serve them up with 4 cups of cooked rice.

1. Place the pork chops in the slow cooker and use a fork to pierce them all over. Sprinkle the onion slices on top of the pork. In a small bowl, whisk together the garlic, soy sauce, vinegar, brown sugar, ginger, and five-spice powder. Pour over the pork chops. Cover and cook on low for 4 hours.

2. About 20 minutes before serving, add the snap peas. Cover and continue cooking until they are crisp-tender. Serve with rice.

TIP: Pork chops are lean, so it's important not to overcook them. A cook time of 4 hours really is quite enough. If you plan on being away from the house for longer than that, substitute a fattier cut, such as country pork ribs, which can cook for 6 to 8 hours.

SZECHUAN BABY BACK RIBS

SERVES 6

PREP
10 MINUTES

COOK
8 TO 10 HOURS
ON LOW

There are two main (and necessary) steps involved in making this dish. First, the baby back ribs are rubbed with a Szechuan mix and steeped in the slow cooker. The second part involves a quick slather of sweet-spicy Asian chile sauce and time under the broiler. That minimal effort results in memorable, tongue-singeing racks with the caramelization and char you seek. If you have Szechuan peppercorns, use them in place of your standard black pepper for an extra kick of flavor.

2 teaspoons freshly ground black pepper

1 teaspoon kosher salt

½ teaspoon ground coriander

½ teaspoon garlic powder

½ teaspoon ground cumin

¼ teaspoon ground ginger

3 pounds baby back ribs, trimmed

½ cup water

1 small onion, sliced

1 garlic clove, minced

½ cup honey

½ cup Sriracha

2½ tablespoons Asian chili sauce (such as sambal oelek)

¼ cup brown sugar

1. In a small bowl, mix together the pepper, salt, coriander, garlic powder, cumin, and ginger. Rub the mix on the ribs. Add the water to the slow cooker, followed by the ribs. Top the meat with the onion and garlic. Cover and cook on low for 8 to 10 hours.

2. Preheat your oven's broiler. In another small bowl, make the glaze by combining the honey, Sriracha, chili sauce, and brown sugar. Gently remove the ribs from the liquid and transfer to an aluminum foil–lined baking sheet. Discard the cooking liquid, onion, and garlic. Generously brush the ribs with the glaze and broil them, watching closely to avoid burning, until caramelized, 3 to 5 minutes. Remove them from the oven and enjoy immediately.

TIP: If you don't want to broil your ribs before serving, they can also be placed in a preheated 375°F oven for 15 minutes. This method requires less oversight from you, making it a good option when you are busy with other things.

SERVES 6

PREP
20 MINUTES

COOK
4 TO 6 HOURS ON LOW

1 tablespoon extra-virgin olive oil

6 (1-inch-thick) sirloin pork chops

1 onion, finely chopped

4 garlic cloves, minced

½ cup dry white wine

2 cups Chicken Stock (page 30) or low-sodium if store-bought

⅓ cup all-purpose flour

½ teaspoon garlic powder

½ teaspoon kosher salt, plus more for seasoning

½ teaspoon freshly ground black pepper, plus more for seasoning

2 bay leaves

1 tablespoon browning sauce, such as Maggi Liquid Seasoning

SMOTHERED PORK CHOPS

This Southern dish is true comfort food. It's pretty simple to make a pan-fried version, but there's something about coming home to the porky smell, with little more to do than lift the lid and dive in. I suggest serving them with a mound of buttery, mashed unpeeled, red potatoes, or Loaded Mashed Potatoes (page 164).

BROWN: In a slow cooker with a stove-top function, or in a Dutch oven or heavy-bottomed pan over medium-high heat, heat the oil until shimmering. Season the chops with salt and pepper, and brown, about 3 minutes per side. Remove and set aside.

1. In the same vessel you browned the meat (or in a new one, if you did not brown, with 1 tablespoon olive oil), add the onion and garlic. Sauté, stirring occasionally, until tender, about 5 minutes. Add the wine and bring to a boil. Simmer for a minute before adding the chicken stock. Whisk in the flour, stirring until no lumps remain.

2. Place the pork chops—with as little overlap as possible—and the sauce in the slow cooker now. Add the garlic powder, salt, pepper, bay leaves, and browning sauce. Stir to combine. Cover and cook on low for 4 to 6 hours.

3. Discard the bay leaves. Season with additional salt and pepper, as needed. Serve, spooning the sauce on top of the chops.

TIP: For a thicker, more down home–style gravy, transfer the gravy from the slow cooker to a medium pan over medium heat on the stove top and whisk in ½ cup of buttermilk and 2 tablespoons of flour. Keep the chops warm, covered on a plate.

HAWAIIAN-STYLE KALUA PIG

SERVES 8

PREP
5 MINUTES

COOK
16 TO 18 HOURS
ON LOW

Who has time to build an *imu*? Not I. That's why, when I need a fix, I make my kalua pig in the slow cooker. If you can get your hands on banana leaves, by all means do; wrapping the pork in them lends a subtly sweet, almost grassy nuance to the meat. Otherwise, proceed without. Just be sure to start this dish the night before, not the morning of. It requires a longer-than-average cooking time to achieve authentic results.

3 frozen banana leaves, thawed (optional)

1 whole (5- to 6-pound) pork butt

1 teaspoon kosher salt, plus more for seasoning

1 tablespoon liquid smoke

2 tablespoons soy sauce

1 cup water

Freshly ground black pepper

1. Lay the banana leaves (if using) in a cross-hatch pattern on a work surface. Place the pork on top of the leaves and pierce it all over with a fork. Rub the meat with the salt, liquid smoke, and soy sauce. Fold the leaves around the pork, enclosing it completely.

2. Place the pork in the slow cooker. Add the water. Cover and cook on low for 16 to 18 hours.

3. Transfer the pork to a cutting board and use two forks to shred the meat. Return the shredded meat to the slow cooker and mix it with its juices to moisten. Season with additional salt and pepper, as needed. Serve immediately.

TIP: While cooking pork shoulder for up to 18 hours seems extravagant, I assure you that in this case it is both appropriate and necessary. Doing so mimics the flavor—and crusty exterior—of Hawaii's celebratory, pit-smoked meal. If you can flip it halfway through the cooking time, so much the better.

SERVES 8

PREP
10 MINUTES

COOK
4 HOURS ON LOW

ITALIAN SAUSAGE SANDWICH
WITH SWEET AND HOT PEPPERS

8 links Italian sausage

2 large red bell peppers, seeded and sliced

1 large green bell pepper, seeded and sliced

3 garlic cloves, thinly sliced

1 large onion, sliced

1 teaspoon balsamic vinegar

6 ounces beer

½ cup Chicken Stock (page 30) or low-sodium if store-bought

½ teaspoon kosher salt, plus more for seasoning

¼ teaspoon freshly ground black pepper, plus more for seasoning

8 hoagie rolls, sliced

1 jar hot giardiniera, as condiment

I like an Italian sausage sandwich as is. Even more, though, I enjoy Chicago-style combos, which include both Chicago-Style Italian Beef (page 67) and Italian sausage. Still, these links are no slouch, especially when served with giardiana (hot pickled vegetables).

1. In the slow cooker, combine the Italian sausage, red bell pepper, bell pepper, garlic, onion, vinegar, beer, chicken stock, salt, and pepper. Cover and cook on low for 4 hours.

2. Season with additional salt and pepper, as needed. Tuck a sausage into each roll and top with peppers, onions, and giardiniera.

TIP: I rarely prepare my Italian sausage with tomato sauce. However, when the bumper crops of vegetables arrive all at once, it's a great time to use produce from the garden. That's where tomatoes come in. Choose some tender ones and either purée them or cut them into wedges and throw them on in there.

BRAZILIAN PORK FEIJOADA

SERVES 8

PREP
5 MINUTES

COOK
8 HOURS ON LOW

A traditional black bean and pork stew, Brazilian pork *feijoada* is best served with white rice. Loaded with porky bits, it's impressive and hearty, yet it doesn't require a great deal of effort on your part. Be mindful that the cooking time of beans varies. They won't be ready in less than 6 hours, for sure, but they may require more than 8 hours. When purchasing a smoked sausage, I look for andouille, though smoked Polish will work fine, too.

1. Put the black beans, chicken stock, pork, ham bone, bacon, sausage, garlic, onion, vinegar, bay leaves, salt, pepper, and cumin in the slow cooker and stir to combine. Cover and cook on low for 8 hours, or until the beans are tender when pierced with a fork.

2. Discard the bay leaves. Use two forks to shred the pork shoulder in the slow cooker. Discard the fatty bits. Season the stew with additional salt and pepper, as needed. Ladle into bowls and serve immediately, or cover and refrigerate for up to 3 days.

TIP: For a dash of color and a burst of brightness, garnish your stew with finely chopped flat-leaf parsley. Serve it with a bowl of wilted greens, such as collards, as a traditional accompaniment. Depending on seasonal availability, chard, kale, or spinach also works well.

1 (16-ounce) package dry black beans, picked over, soaked overnight, drained, and rinsed

7 cups Chicken Stock (page 30) or low-sodium if store-bought

1 pound boneless pork shoulder, in one piece

1 leftover ham bone (see 85)

4 thick-cut bacon slices, finely chopped

½ pound smoked sausage, diced

4 garlic cloves, minced

1 medium onion, finely chopped

1½ teaspoons red wine vinegar

3 bay leaves

2 teaspoons kosher salt, plus more for seasoning

½ teaspoon freshly ground black pepper, plus more for seasoning

½ teaspoon ground cumin

LAMB STEW WITH CHERRY TOMATOES AND CILANTRO (PAGE 102)

5

LAMB

WHETHER YOU LOVE IT OR FIND
yourself too intimidated to cook it, lamb deserves a spot on
your dinner table—and not just on Easter or Passover or special
occasions. Lending itself to both slow cooker "stir-fries" and global
main courses your whole family will love, it's a worthy alternative
to beef, pork, and chicken, one with enough oomph to stand up to
boldly flavored sauces and seasonings. Give it a go with these easy,
flavor-rich dishes, which aim to sate your cravings or win you over—
whatever the case may be.

1 tablespoon extra-virgin olive oil

2½ pounds trimmed boned lamb shoulder, cut into 1½- to 2-inch pieces

1 teaspoon kosher salt, plus more for seasoning

1 large onion, finely chopped

2 garlic cloves, minced

1 tablespoon tomato paste

2 cups Chicken Stock (page 30) or low-sodium if store-bought

2 cinnamon sticks

2 teaspoons freshly grated lemon zest

1 tablespoon ground cumin

2 teaspoons ground coriander

½ teaspoon ground fennel

8 ounces cherry tomatoes

¼ cup finely chopped fresh cilantro, for garnish

LAMB STEW
WITH CHERRY TOMATOES AND CILANTRO

Warming and hearty, this lamb stew pops with flavor thanks to cilantro and juicy cherry tomatoes added toward the end of cooking to retain their shape. I like to cut the richness of this stew with a dollop of lemon and parsley-flecked plain yogurt—especially when it's bolstered by a little garlic and black pepper. Give it a whirl.

BROWN: In a slow cooker with a stove-top function, or in a Dutch oven or heavy-bottomed pan over medium-high heat, heat the oil until shimmering. Season the lamb with salt and pepper and brown on all sides, about 5 minutes.

1. Put the lamb in the slow cooker, along with the onion, garlic, tomato paste, chicken stock, cinnamon sticks, lemon zest, cumin, coriander, fennel, and salt, and stir to combine. Cover and cook on low for 8 hours.

2. About 30 minutes before serving, add the cherry tomatoes. Cover and continue cooking until warmed through. Discard the cinnamon sticks. Season the stew with additional salt, as needed. Ladle the stew into bowls and garnish with the cilantro before serving.

TIP: Serve this dish with couscous on the side. I especially like Israeli couscous for its larger size and chewier texture. When preparing it, you'll get the best results if you toast it in a little bit of olive oil before cooking. Follow the quantities on the package directions, use chicken stock instead of water, and finish the couscous with a sprinkle of chopped flat-leaf parsley.

GARLICKY LEG OF LAMB
WITH LEMON

SERVES 6

PREP
15 MINUTES

COOK
6 TO 8 HOURS ON LOW

Lamb, garlic, and lemon are a match made in heaven. Add a bit of herbaceous Italian seasoning into the mix and the combination of familiar ingredients somehow seems special. I like to serve this dish with oven-roasted potatoes, though you can add some waxy potato wedges in with the lamb to make a one-pot meal.

BROWN: In a slow cooker with a stove-top function, or in a Dutch oven or heavy-bottomed pan over medium-high heat, heat the oil until shimmering. Season the lamb with salt and pepper, and brown on all sides, about 5 minutes total.

1. Put the lamb in the slow cooker. Add the onion, garlic, salt, pepper, Italian seasoning, chicken stock, wine, and lemon. Stir to combine and spoon over the roast. Cover and cook on low for 6 to 8 hours.

2. Season the roast with additional salt and pepper, as desired. Transfer the lamb to a cutting board and let it rest for 15 minutes before carving.

3. Use a fine-mesh sieve or cheesecloth-lined colander to strain the braising liquid into a medium saucepan. Discard the solids. Whisk in the flour until no lumps remain, and bring the mixture to a rolling boil on the stove top. Continue whisking until it reaches a gravy-like thickness. Carve the meat and serve with the gravy.

1½ tablespoons extra-virgin olive oil

1 (5-pound) bone-in leg of lamb

1 small onion, sliced

4 garlic cloves, sliced

½ teaspoon kosher salt, plus more for seasoning

½ teaspoon freshly ground black pepper, plus more for seasoning

½ teaspoon Italian seasoning

½ cup Chicken Stock (page 30) or low-sodium if store-bought

¼ cup white wine

½ lemon, thinly sliced with seeds removed

2 tablespoons all-purpose flour

TOMATO-ROSEMARY BRAISED LAMB SHANKS WITH CHICKPEAS

SERVES 4

PREP
15 MINUTES

COOK
8 HOURS ON LOW

When slowly simmered and braised in bold, red wine–inflected tomato sauce, lamb shanks become lush and tender. They're impressive to look at and even more so to taste, not to mention a winning choice atop a mountain of garlicky mashed potatoes or soft, creamy polenta. Go all out and finish your dish with an easy-to-prepare gremolata—a paste of minced garlic, lemon zest, and salt mixed with chopped flat-leaf parsley and a little olive oil.

BROWN: In a slow cooker with a stove-top function, or in a Dutch oven or heavy-bottomed pan over medium-high heat, heat the oil until shimmering. Season the lamb shanks with salt and pepper, and brown on all sides, about 5 minutes total. Transfer the meat to a plate and reserve. Add the wine and bring to a boil, scraping up the browned bits from the bottom of the pan. Simmer for a minute to evaporate the alcohol.

1. Put the browned lamb shanks along with the pan juices in the slow cooker. If you skipped browning, place the lamb shanks in the slow cooker along with the wine (reduced to ½ cup). Add in the tomatoes, carrots, celery, onion, garlic, chicken stock, rosemary, and pepper. Stir to combine. Cover and cook on low for 8 hours. ➤

2 tablespoons extra-virgin olive oil

4 lamb shanks (about 1 pound each), trimmed of fat

¾ cup dry red wine

2 (28-ounce) cans tomatoes

2 carrots, peeled and chopped

2 celery stalks, chopped

1 medium onion, chopped

4 garlic cloves, minced

1½ cups Chicken Stock (page 30) or low-sodium if store-bought

1½ teaspoons dried rosemary, crumbled

½ teaspoon freshly ground black pepper, plus more for seasoning

1 (15-ounce) can chickpeas, drained and rinsed

Kosher salt

2. About 30 minutes before the end of the cooking time, add the chickpeas. Cover and continue cooking until warmed through. Transfer the shanks to a platter and cover with aluminum foil to keep warm. Using an immersion blender, purée the sauce or transfer to a blender and purée until smooth. Season the dish with additional salt and pepper, as needed. Spoon the sauce over the lamb shanks and serve.

TIP: Pair this hearty dish with a bottle of dry, plummy, plush red wine, such as one made with Monastrell grapes.

EASTER LAMB

SERVES 6

PREP
15 MINUTES

COOK
6 TO 8 HOURS ON LOW

There's no reason to relegate this dish to the holidays. This zippy take on Easter Lamb gets its piquant flavor from Dijon mustard. The red wine sauce is infused with meaty flavor during cooking and then thickened on the stove top prior to serving.

BROWN: In a slow cooker with a stove-top function, or in a Dutch oven or heavy-bottomed pan over medium-high heat, heat the oil until shimmering. Season the lamb with salt and pepper, then rub with the mustard. Place in the slow cooker or pan and brown on all sides, about 5 minutes total.

1. Put the lamb (rubbed with the mustard if you skipped browning) in the slow cooker. Add the onion, garlic, salt, pepper, wine, and chicken stock. Stir to combine. Cover and cook on low for 6 to 8 hours.

2. Taste and season the lamb with additional salt and pepper, as needed. Transfer the lamb to a cutting board and let it rest for 15 minutes before carving.

3. Use a fine-mesh sieve or cheesecloth-lined colander to strain the braising liquid into a medium saucepan; discard the solids. Whisk in the flour until no lumps remain, and bring the mixture to a rolling boil on the stove top. Continue whisking until it reaches a gravy-like thickness. Carve the meat and serve with the gravy.

TIP: To take this dish to the next level, serve it with a spring-like side such as minted peas or fava beans laced with dill. And whip up a quick condiment by mixing sour cream, lemon zest, finely chopped mint, and grated horseradish.

1½ tablespoons extra-virgin olive oil

1 (5-pound) bone-in leg of lamb

2 tablespoons Dijon mustard

1 small onion, sliced

4 garlic cloves, sliced

½ teaspoon kosher salt, plus more for seasoning

½ teaspoon freshly ground black pepper, plus more for seasoning

¼ cup red wine

½ cup Chicken Stock (page 30) or low-sodium if store-bought

2 tablespoons all-purpose flour

SERVES 6

PREP
15 MINUTES

COOK
6 TO 8 HOURS ON LOW

1½ tablespoons extra-virgin olive oil

1 (5-pound) bone-in leg of lamb

1 small onion, sliced

4 garlic cloves, sliced

½ teaspoon kosher salt, plus more for seasoning

½ teaspoon freshly ground black pepper, plus more for seasoning

½ teaspoon dried oregano, preferably Mediterranean

2 bay leaves

½ cup Chicken Stock (page 30) or low-sodium if store-bought

¼ cup white wine

½ lemon, thinly sliced, seeds removed

¼ cup Kalamata olives, pitted and sliced

2 tablespoons all-purpose flour

GREEK LAMB
WITH OREGANO AND OLIVES

Rich and a bit gamey, lamb is often treated as a special-occasion meat. However, there's no reason it should be, since it's easy to prepare any day of the week. When paired with Greek flavors (oregano and Kalamata olives, to be exact), this simple dish is elevated to new and welcome heights.

BROWN: In a slow cooker with a stove-top function, or in a Dutch oven or heavy-bottomed pan over medium-high heat, heat the oil until shimmering. Season the lamb with salt and pepper, and brown on all sides, about 5 minutes total.

1. Put the lamb in the slow cooker, along with the onion, garlic, salt, pepper, oregano, bay leaves, chicken stock, wine, and lemon slices. Stir to combine and spoon over the roast. Cover and cook on low for 6 to 8 hours.

2. About 30 minutes before serving, add the olives. Cover and continue cooking. Season the dish with additional salt and pepper, as needed. Transfer the lamb to a cutting board and let it rest for 15 minutes before carving.

3. Discard the bay leaves. Use a fine-mesh sieve or cheesecloth-lined colander to strain the braising liquid into a medium saucepan. Discard the solids. Whisk in the flour until no lumps remain, and bring the mixture to a rolling boil on the stove top. Add the solids back in and continue whisking until it reaches a gravy-like thickness.

4. Carve the meat and serve with the gravy.

TIP: If at all possible, take your lamb out of the refrigerator an hour before cooking. If you don't want to brown it in a pan, rub the meat with olive oil, season it with salt and pepper, and broil it in a preheated oven for about 5 minutes per side.

SERVES 6

PREP
15 MINUTES

COOK
6 TO 8 HOURS ON LOW

1½ tablespoons extra-virgin olive oil

1 (6-pound) bone-in lamb shoulder

4 garlic cloves, thinly sliced

2 medium onions, sliced

3 carrots, peeled and cut into large chunks

2 parsnips, peeled and cut into large chunks

1 large turnip, peeled and cut into large wedges

2 bay leaves

½ teaspoon kosher salt, plus more for seasoning

½ teaspoon freshly ground black pepper, plus more for seasoning

½ cup Chicken Stock (page 30) or low-sodium if store-bought

¼ cup white wine

2 tablespoons all-purpose flour

LAMB SHOULDER
WITH SMASHED ROOT VEGETABLES

Root vegetables just don't get enough love, but here a mixed mash of them plays a significant supporting role to garlicky lamb shoulder. To infuse the meat with even more flavor, pierce it with a knife in several places and insert the garlic slivers. By doing so, you'll also flavor the sauce—a win-win.

BROWN: In a slow cooker with a stove-top function, or in a Dutch oven or heavy-bottomed pan over medium-high heat, heat the oil until shimmering. Season the lamb with salt and pepper, and brown on all sides, about 5 minutes total.

1. Put the lamb in the slow cooker. Scatter the garlic, onions, carrots, parsnips, turnip, and bay leaves around the sides of the roast. Sprinkle the meat and vegetables with the salt and pepper. Pour the chicken stock and wine evenly over the top. Cover and cook on low for 6 to 8 hours.

2. Discard the bay leaves. Season the dish with additional salt and pepper, as needed. Transfer the lamb to a cutting board and let it rest for 15 minutes. Meanwhile, transfer the vegetables to a large bowl and smash lightly with a fork or potato masher, leaving some texture.

3. Use a fine-mesh sieve or cheesecloth-lined colander to strain the braising liquid into a medium saucepan. Discard the solids. Whisk in the flour until no lumps remain, and bring the gravy to a rolling boil on the stove top. Continue whisking until it reaches a gravy-like thickness.

4. Carve the lamb. Serve with the root vegetables and gravy.

TIP: Don't carve the lamb before it has a chance to rest. Otherwise, the meat juices will escape and you'll lose the lush richness you waited all day to achieve.

SERVES 6

PREP
15 MINUTES

COOK
6 TO 8 HOURS ON LOW

1½ tablespoons extra-virgin olive oil

1 (6-pound) bone-in lamb shoulder

1 cup dry red wine

12 garlic cloves, left whole

2 medium onions, cut into wedges

3 carrots, peeled and cut into large chunks

1 tablespoon freshly grated lemon zest

½ teaspoon dried rosemary, crumbled

½ teaspoon dried thyme

½ teaspoon kosher salt, plus more for seasoning

½ teaspoon freshly ground black pepper, plus more for seasoning

1 cup Chicken Stock (page 30) or low-sodium if store-bought

2 tablespoons all-purpose flour

RED WINE-BRAISED LAMB SHOULDER

Although the supporting ingredients—wine, garlic, carrots, onions—are familiar, when combined with lamb they make this main course something special. The nuanced, herb-spiked gravy gets extra flavor from braising the meat low and slow.

BROWN: In a slow cooker with a stove-top function, or in a Dutch oven or heavy-bottomed pan over medium-high heat, heat the oil until shimmering. Season the lamb with salt and pepper, and brown on all sides, about 5 minutes total. Add the wine and bring to a boil. Simmer for a minute to evaporate the alcohol.

1. Put the lamb in the slow cooker, along with the wine, garlic, onions, carrots, lemon zest, rosemary, thyme, salt, pepper, and chicken stock. Stir to combine and spoon some of the wine mixture over the top of the lamb. Cover and cook on low for 6 to 8 hours.

2. Discard the bay leaves. Season with additional salt and pepper, as needed. Transfer the lamb and vegetables to a cutting board, and let them rest for 15 minutes under an aluminum-foil tent to keep warm.

3. Use a fine-mesh sieve or cheesecloth-lined colander to strain the braising liquid into a medium saucepan. Discard the solids. Whisk in the flour until no lumps remain, then bring the mixture to a rolling boil on the stove top. Continue whisking until it reaches a gravy-like thickness.

4. Carve the lamb and serve with the vegetables and gravy.

TIP: To really boost the flavor of the meat, marinate it in the wine, garlic, herbs, and onion the night before. Pat it dry before browning and reserve the marinade, using it to deglaze the pan, then use it in the recipe as called for.

SERVES 6

PREP
15 MINUTES

COOK
6 TO 8 HOURS ON LOW

1½ tablespoons extra-virgin olive oil

1 (4-pound) bone-in lamb shoulder or neck

1 large onion

4 garlic cloves, minced

1 teaspoon sweet paprika

1 teaspoon ground cumin

2 cinnamon sticks

½ cup Chicken Stock (page 30) or low-sodium if store-bought

½ teaspoon kosher salt, plus more for seasoning

½ teaspoon freshly ground black pepper, plus more for seasoning

1 cup green olives, pitted and sliced

1 cup dried apricots, sliced

2 tablespoons all-purpose flour

Cooked couscous, for serving

BONE-IN LAMB
WITH APRICOTS AND GREEN OLIVES

Fragrantly spiced, this inviting, Moroccan-inspired lamb dish is the sort you can save for when company comes over, but you'll surely want to cook it for family dinner, too. Serve it with a side of couscous (I like the large-pearl Israeli kind) and a pot of piping hot mint tea.

BROWN: In a slow cooker with a stove-top function, or in a Dutch oven or heavy-bottomed pan over medium-high heat, heat the oil until shimmering. Season the lamb with salt and pepper, and brown on all sides, about 5 minutes total. Add the onion and garlic and continue cooking for 3 minutes.

1. Put the lamb, onion, and garlic in the slow cooker. Add the paprika, cumin, cinnamon sticks, chicken stock, salt, and pepper. Stir to combine. Cover and cook on low for 6 to 8 hours.

2. About 30 minutes before serving, add the olives and apricots. Cover and continue cooking. Season with additional salt and pepper, as needed. Discard the cinnamon sticks and transfer the lamb to a cutting board, letting it rest for 15 minutes before carving.

3. Use a fine-mesh sieve or cheesecloth-lined colander to strain the braising liquid into a medium saucepan. Reserve the olives and apricots. Whisk in the flour until no lumps remain, and bring the mixture to a rolling boil on the stove top. Continue whisking until it reaches a gravy-like thickness.

4. Carve the meat and pour the gravy into a serving bowl. Serve the lamb on a platter of couscous, topped with the reserved olives and apricots.

TIP: For a tasty sandwich the next day, stuff a crusty baguette with shredded leftovers, moistening the bread with a bit of the savory, slightly sweet gravy.

SERVES 6

PREP
15 MINUTES

COOK
6 TO 8 HOURS ON LOW

STICKY CUMIN LAMB

This Xinjiang dish, which often appears on Chinese, Hunan, and Szechuan menus alike, has a pleasing kick and loads of smoky flavor. For an even richer dish, marinate the lamb in a mixture of vegetable oil, cumin, hot chiles, soy sauce, sugar, and garlic the night before. Pat the meat dry before browning it.

1 tablespoon extra-virgin olive oil

½ tablespoon sesame oil

2 pounds boneless lamb shoulder, cut into ½-inch-by-2-inch strips

1 large onion, sliced

2 garlic cloves, minced

½ cup Chicken Stock (page 30) or low-sodium if store-bought

2 teaspoons soy sauce

2 tablespoons ground cumin

1 tablespoon packed brown sugar

1 tablespoon Chinese black vinegar, or white vinegar

½ teaspoon red pepper flakes

½ teaspoon kosher salt, plus more for seasoning

1½ teaspoons cornstarch

3 cups cooked white rice, for serving

3 scallions, white and green parts sliced, for garnish

BROWN: In a slow cooker with a stove-top function, or in a Dutch oven or heavy-bottomed pan over medium-high heat, heat the olive oil and the sesame oil until shimmering. Season the lamb shoulder with salt and pepper, and brown on all sides, about 5 minutes total.

1. Put the lamb in the slow cooker, along with the onion and garlic. In a medium bowl, whisk together the sesame oil (if you didn't brown the lamb), chicken stock, soy sauce, cumin, brown sugar, vinegar, red pepper flakes, and salt. Pour over the lamb. Cover and cook on low for 6 to 8 hours.

2. Season with additional salt, as needed. About 30 minutes before serving, whisk in the cornstarch, taking care that there are no lumps. Cover and continue cooking until the sauce is thickened. Serve atop the rice, garnished with the scallions.

TIP: For added flavor and visual appeal, garnish the dish with chopped cilantro, also called Chinese parsley, along with the scallions.

LAMB VINDALOO

SERVES 6

PREP
15 MINUTES

COOK
6 TO 8 HOURS ON LOW

Your house will smell like curry, for a day or two, at least, when you make this dish. If you ask me, that's a good thing. When served with fluffy basmati rice to sop up the savory sauce, it's a spice-lover's dream. A finishing shower of cilantro both brightens the dish and cuts through the richness of the meat.

BROWN: In a slow cooker with a stove-top function, or in a Dutch oven or heavy-bottomed pan over medium-high heat, heat the oil until shimmering. Season the lamb with salt and pepper, and brown on all sides, about 5 minutes total.

1. Put the lamb in the slow cooker, along with the onion, garlic, bay leaves, salt, pepper, coriander, turmeric, cardamom, potatoes, chicken stock, and vinegar. Stir to combine. Cover and cook on low for 6 to 8 hours.

2. About 30 minutes before serving, discard the bay leaves. Season with additional salt and pepper, as needed. Whisk in the flour, taking care there are no lumps, cover, and continue cooking until the sauce thickens.

3. Garnish with the cilantro before serving.

TIP: For the most authentic flavor, brown your lamb in ghee, which is clarified butter that can be made from skimming the foam from the top of melted butter. It can also be purchased from the shelves of well-stocked grocery stores and Asian markets.

1½ tablespoons extra-virgin olive oil

2 pounds boneless lamb shoulder, cut into 1-inch cubes

1 teaspoon kosher salt, plus more for seasoning

½ teaspoon freshly ground black pepper, plus more for seasoning

1 small onion, finely chopped

4 garlic cloves, minced

2 bay leaves

1 teaspoon ground coriander

½ teaspoon ground turmeric

¼ teaspoon ground cardamom

12 waxy baby potatoes, such as Yukon Gold

1½ cups Chicken Stock (page 30) or low-sodium if store-bought

2 teaspoons apple cider vinegar

2 tablespoons all-purpose flour

¼ cup minced cilantro, for garnish

COQ AU VIN (PAGE 129)

6
POULTRY

WHICH PROTEIN WOULD YOU

choose if you could choose only one? Most people would answer poultry, chicken in particular. Why? It's versatile and lean but can also, depending on the cut, produce rich results. It's no wonder it's a favorite across cultures, featuring in some of the world's most beloved dishes—mine included! Dark meat especially lends itself well to slow cooking, with classics like Chicken Noodle Soup (page 125) and Chicken and Dumplings (page 127), or warming Thai Red Curry Chicken (page 132).

2 pounds boneless, skinless chicken thighs

8 chicken drumsticks, skinned

40 cloves (about 3 heads) garlic, peeled

1 large onion, chopped

1½ cups Chicken Stock (page 30) or low-sodium if store-bought

½ cup dry vermouth

2 bay leaves

½ teaspoon kosher salt, plus more for seasoning

½ teaspoon freshly ground black pepper, plus more for seasoning

¼ teaspoon ground nutmeg

2 tablespoons all-purpose flour

¼ cup heavy (whipping) cream

CHICKEN WITH 40 CLOVES OF GARLIC

Forty cloves of garlic—vampires beware! I know it seems like a lot, but believe me when I say it mellows significantly during cooking, melting into a gentle complement to the tender, slow-cooked chicken. White wine can be substituted for vermouth, though vermouth is certainly punchier, so if you have it, I recommend using it.

1. Put the chicken thighs and drumsticks in the slow cooker, along with the garlic, onion, chicken stock, vermouth, bay leaves, salt, pepper, and nutmeg. Stir to combine and then coat the chicken. Cover and cook on low for 6 to 8 hours.

2. About 45 minutes before serving, whisk together the flour and heavy cream in a small bowl until no lumps remain. Add to the slow cooker, and cover most of the way, leaving the lid slightly ajar. Continue cooking until the sauce thickens. Discard the bay leaves. Season with additional salt and pepper, as needed. Serve, spooning the sauce over the chicken.

TIP: Because the chicken itself does not impart a great deal of flavor, be sure to season this dish generously. However, add salt and pepper a little at a time because adding spices is easy; over-seasoning, on the other hand, can quickly ruin the dish.

CHICKEN TORTILLA SOUP

SERVES 6

PREP
15 MINUTES

COOK
8 HOURS ON LOW

What's not to love about a bowl of chicken tortilla soup? It's comforting and yet ideal for serving at a celebration. It's familiar and highly customizable. It simply has the makings of a great meal and is a great option when serving a lot of people. Put the toppings in bowls and let guests gussy up their soup to suit their individual tastes. Don't let the long ingredients list put you off—chances are you already have on hand all but a couple of the ingredients.

1. Put the chicken in the slow cooker, along with the onion, garlic, jalapeño, chili powder, cumin, salt, pepper, tomatoes, tomato paste, vinegar, Worcestershire sauce, hot sauce, and chicken stock. Stir to combine. Cover and cook on low for 8 hours.

2. Use two forks to shred the chicken inside the slow cooker. Season with additional salt and pepper, as needed. Ladle the soup into bowls and garnish with your choice of tortilla chips, cilantro, sour cream, avocado, and a squirt of lime.

TIP: This spicy dish welcomes a good cerveza—think Dos Equis—to tame the flames (especially if you are like me and add extra minced habañero to your soup).

1½ pounds boneless, skinless chicken thighs

1 medium onion, finely chopped

3 garlic cloves, minced

1 large jalapeño pepper, finely chopped

1½ teaspoons chili powder, preferably ancho

1½ teaspoons ground cumin

1 teaspoon kosher salt, plus more for seasoning

½ teaspoon freshly ground black pepper, plus more for seasoning

1 (28-ounce) can crushed tomatoes

1 tablespoon tomato paste

2 teaspoons apple cider vinegar

1½ teaspoons Worcestershire sauce

1½ teaspoons hot sauce, such as Tabasco

6 cups Chicken Stock (page 30) or low-sodium if store-bought

GARNISH OPTIONS

1 cup crushed tortilla chips, ½ cup chopped fresh cilantro, ½ cup sour cream, 1 avocado, diced, 1 lime, cut into wedges

1 large onion, thinly sliced

3 pounds boneless, skinless chicken thighs

1 teaspoon kosher salt, plus more for seasoning

1 teaspoon freshly ground pepper, plus more for seasoning

½ cup all-purpose flour

2 (4.5-ounce) cans tomato paste

1 green bell pepper, seeded and finely chopped

4 ounces fresh or canned mushrooms

3 tablespoons capers, drained and rinsed

4 garlic cloves, minced

3 teaspoons Italian seasoning

1 teaspoon red pepper flakes

½ cup dry white wine

CHICKEN CACCIATORE

Cacciatore is Italian for "hunter." This popular dish sports a robust tomato sauce with near-endless variations. Yet one thing remains constant: it's a welcome, family-friendly dish you can proudly serve to company. The recipe makes a lot of sauce. Serve this chicken dish over pasta, or even with rice or bread to enjoy every tasty bit.

1. Cover the bottom of the slow cooker bowl with the onion slices. Season the chicken with the salt and pepper, rub with the flour, shaking off any excess, and place the chicken on top of the onion.

2. In a medium bowl, combine the tomato paste, bell pepper, mushrooms, capers, garlic, Italian seasoning, red pepper flakes, and white wine. Stir to combine. Pour the mixture over the chicken. Cover and cook on low for 6 hours.

3. Taste and season with additional salt and pepper, if needed. Serve immediately.

TIP: For even better results, incorporate ½ ounce of dried mushrooms such as porcini. To rehydrate them, place the dried mushrooms in a heatproof bowl and top with 2 cups of boiling water. Let sit for 15 to 30 minutes, until the mushrooms have softened. Drain, rinse until the water runs clear, and add them to the slow cooker.

CHICKEN GUMBO

SERVES 6

PREP
10 MINUTES

COOK
8 HOURS ON LOW

I don't know about you, but I welcome a bit of heat and often add more hot sauce to suit my taste. You can reduce the heat in this recipe by using a Louisiana-style hot sauce, such as the aptly named Louisiana Hot Sauce, in place of the Tabasco. A bed of rice beneath also helps cool the burn, not to mention fill out the meal. About 3 cups of cooked rice should do for this recipe.

1. Put the chicken in the slow cooker, along with the celery, onion, bell pepper, garlic, Creole seasoning, salt, bay leaves, chicken stock, Worcestershire sauce, and hot sauce. Stir to combine. Cover and cook on low for 8 hours.

2. Discard the bay leaves. Season with additional salt and pepper, as needed. Ladle into bowls and serve.

TIP: This gumbo can be stored in an airtight container in the refrigerator for up to 4 days or frozen for 6 months.

1 pound boneless, skinless chicken thighs

1 celery stalk, chopped

1 medium onion, chopped

½ cup diced green bell pepper

2 garlic cloves, minced

1 tablespoon Creole seasoning

½ teaspoon kosher salt, plus more for seasoning

3 bay leaves

6 cups Chicken Stock (page 30) or low-sodium if store-bought

1½ teaspoons Worcestershire sauce

1 teaspoon hot sauce, such as Tabasco

Freshly ground black pepper

CHICKEN NOODLE SOUP

SERVES 6

PREP
15 MINUTES

COOK
8 HOURS ON LOW

Everybody's favorite, get-well-soon chicken noodle soup must have dozens of variations. This version keeps the traditional flavors intact, while offering up a burst of flavor from fresh lemon juice, along with the healing power of spinach. If you've never had it this way, you're in for a revelation.

1. Put the chicken in the slow cooker, along with the celery, carrot, onion, garlic, chicken stock, bay leaves, salt, pepper, and poultry seasoning. Stir to combine. Cover and cook on low for 8 hours.

2. About 1 hour before serving, shred the chicken from the bones and discard the bones. Add the spinach and egg noodles. Cover and continue cooking cooking until the noodles are tender. Discard the bay leaves. Season with additional salt and pepper, as needed. Ladle into bowls and garnish with the parsley and a squirt of lemon.

TIP: To make this recipe even simpler, replace the raw chicken with a whole rotisserie chicken. Then follow the rest of the recipe as written.

1½ pounds bone-in chicken thighs and drumsticks, skinned

1 celery stalk, finely chopped

1 large carrot, finely chopped

1 medium onion, finely chopped

2 garlic cloves, minced

6 cups Chicken Stock (page 30) or low-sodium if store-bought

2 bay leaves

1 teaspoon kosher salt, plus more for seasoning

½ teaspoon freshly ground black pepper, plus more for seasoning

½ teaspoon poultry seasoning

4 ounces uncooked egg noodles

1 (10-ounce) package chopped, frozen spinach, thawed

¼ cup minced flat-leaf parsley, for garnish

1 lemon, cut into wedges, for garnish

SERVES 6

PREP
10 MINUTES

COOK
4 HOURS ON LOW

Cooking spray or
1 tablespoon extra-virgin
olive oil

2 garlic cloves, minced

1 cup orange marmalade

⅓ cup cornstarch

1 tablespoon rice vinegar

1½ teaspoons soy sauce

1 teaspoon sesame oil

½ teaspoon kosher salt,
plus more for seasoning

½ teaspoon freshly ground
black pepper, plus more
for seasoning

¼ teaspoon red
pepper flakes

2 pounds boneless, skinless
chicken breasts, cut into
½-inch pieces

3 cups cooked white rice,
for serving

2 tablespoons sesame
seeds, lightly toasted,
for garnish

ORANGE CHICKEN

Forget takeout—this to-go standby is easy to prepare at home. Sticky, sweet, *and* tangy, it gets its *oomph* from a mix of marmalade and rice vinegar. The soy sauce gives it a salty kick while a touch of sesame oil lends subtle nuttiness. Just be sure to spray your slow cooker or use a liner before preparing this one—it'll save you cleanup in the end.

1. Use the cooking spray or olive oil to coat the inside (bottom and sides) of the slow cooker. Add the garlic, marmalade, cornstarch, vinegar, soy sauce, sesame oil, salt, pepper, and red pepper flakes and whisk to combine. Add the chicken and stir to coat. Cover and cook on low for 4 hours.

2. Season with additional salt and pepper, as needed. Scoop the rice onto individual plates, spoon the chicken on top, garnish with the sesame seeds and serve immediately.

TIP: Virtually any kind of white rice will work as a side dish, be it long-grain or jasmine.

CHICKEN AND DUMPLINGS

SERVES 6

PREP
20 MINUTES

COOK
8 HOURS ON LOW

When I was a little girl, my mom used to let me choose what dish I wanted her to make on my birthday. Chicken and dumplings is what I asked for most often. Was it the chicken? No. I blame the dumplings for winning me over. She usually made it in a Dutch oven, but the dish effortlessly translates to the slow cooker. Just remember to vent the machine so the biscuits cook properly, by propping up one side of the lid once you drop the biscuits in, so they cook properly.

1. Put the chicken thighs and drumsticks in the slow cooker, along with the carrots, celery, onion, chicken stock, salt, pepper, and bay leaves. Stir to combine. Cover and cook on low for 8 hours.

2. About 30 minutes before serving, discard the bay leaves. Use two forks to shred the chicken inside the slow cooker, and discard the bones from the drumsticks. Add the heavy cream and season with additional salt and pepper, as needed.

3. In a medium bowl, combine the baking mix and milk and stir together just until thoroughly combined, without overmixing. Drop the batter by the heaping tablespoonful into the soup. Cover with the lid, leaving it vented, and continue cooking until the dumplings are no longer raw in the center. Serve.

TIP: Jazz up the dumplings by adding a handful or two of your favorite combination of ingredients, such as black pepper, Cheddar, and chives, to the uncooked batter.

4 boneless, skinless chicken thighs

1 pound chicken drumsticks, skinned

2 carrots, peeled and finely chopped

1 celery stalk, finely chopped

1 medium onion, finely chopped

6 cups Chicken Stock (page 30) or low-sodium if store-bought

½ teaspoon kosher salt, plus more for seasoning

½ teaspoon freshly ground black pepper, plus more for seasoning

2 bay leaves

½ cup heavy (whipping) cream

2 cups all-purpose baking mix

⅔ cup whole milk

SERVES 6

PREP
10 MINUTES

COOK
8 HOURS ON LOW

CHICKEN SAUSAGE AND KALE SOUP

1 tablespoon extra-virgin olive oil

1 pound chicken sausage, casings removed

1 large yellow onion, finely chopped

2 garlic cloves, minced

1 (15.5-ounce) can cannellini beans

1 teaspoon kosher salt, plus more for seasoning

½ teaspoon freshly ground black pepper, plus more for seasoning

2 bay leaves

1 leftover Parmesan cheese rind, plus ½ cup grated Parmesan for garnish

1 bunch kale, cleaned, stemmed, ribbed, and leaves roughly chopped

I'll admit that I can be suspicious of certain kinds of meat—especially versions masquerading as something I love. Even though chicken sausage sports a different, milder flavor than pork or beef, it works really well in this soup. Paired with kale, it's a lighter option when you want to take a break from ultra-rich soups and stews.

BROWN: In a slow cooker with a stove-top function, or in a Dutch oven or heavy-bottomed pan over medium-high heat, heat the oil until shimmering. Season the sausage with salt and pepper, and brown, breaking up the meat into small bits until it is thoroughly cooked.

1. Put the chicken sausage in the slow cooker, along with the onion, garlic, beans, salt, pepper, bay leaves, and Parmesan rind. Stir to combine. Cover and cook on low for 8 hours.

2. During the last 30 minutes of cooking, discard the bay leaves and Parmesan rind. Add the kale. Season with additional salt and pepper, as needed, and continue cooking until the kale is tender. Ladle the soup into bowls and garnish with the Parmesan before serving.

TIP: Kale can be replaced with virtually any green, be it spinach, collards, or mustard greens. Collards and mustard greens are more bitter than kale and need a longer cooking time. Give them 45 minutes to 1 hour to reach perfection.

COQ AU VIN

SERVES 6

PREP
15 MINUTES

COOK
8 HOURS ON LOW

Coq au vin is a classic French dish. Rather than mess too much with an icon, this slightly simplified, slow cooker version keeps fairly true to the original, with red wine for richness, bacon for smokiness, and fresh herbs and garlic. I recommend taking the bit of extra time to make the sauce first.

BROWN: In a slow cooker with a stove-top function, or in a Dutch oven or heavy-bottomed pan over medium-high heat, add the bacon and cook, stirring occasionally, until browned. Move the bacon to the side. Add the chicken and brown, about 3 minutes per side. Add the red wine, then bring to a boil and simmer for 1 minute to evaporate the alcohol.

1. If browned outside the slow cooker, add the bacon, chicken, and wine in the slow cooker now, along with the chicken stock, carrots, onions, garlic, thyme, salt, and pepper. Cover and cook on low for 8 hours.

2. During the last hour or two of cooking, discard the thyme. In a small bowl, whisk together the flour and water, taking care that no lumps remain. Add the flour mixture to the slow cooker, along with the mushrooms. Stir to combine. Cover and continue cooking until the liquid in the slow cooker has thickened and the mushrooms are tender.

TIP: Mushrooms and slow cookers don't exactly go hand-in-hand because, frankly, the mushrooms get rubbery. For the best results, take an extra step and sauté them in butter on the stove top before adding them to your dish at the end of the cooking time.

4 bacon slices, finely chopped

6 boneless, skinless chicken thighs

1½ cups dry red wine

1½ cups Chicken Stock (page 30) or low-sodium if store-bought

½ pound carrots, peeled and cut diagonally into 1-inch pieces

18 pearl onions, peeled

3 garlic cloves, minced

4 fresh thyme sprigs

1 teaspoon kosher salt

½ teaspoon freshly ground black pepper

2 tablespoons all-purpose flour

2 tablespoons water

½ pound mushrooms, cut into thick slices

2 pounds boneless, skinless chicken thighs, cut into 1-inch cubes

1 cup puréed tomatoes

½ cup Chicken Stock (page 30) or low-sodium if store-bought

¼ cup heavy (whipping) cream

2 tablespoons freshly squeezed lemon juice

2 teaspoons ground cumin

2 teaspoons freshly ground black pepper, plus more for seasoning

1 teaspoon ground cinnamon

1 teaspoon kosher salt, plus more for seasoning

½ teaspoon cayenne pepper

1 garlic clove, minced

1-inch knob fresh ginger

1 cup plain yogurt

CHICKEN TIKKA MASALA

Chicken tikka masala is a dish of somewhat uncertain origin. What *is* certain is that it is a favorite in the United Kingdom (where it is claimed as their own), and a growing favorite here in the United States. Fortunately, it can be made easily at home. In fact, you probably already have most, if not all the spices in your pantry.

1. Put the chicken in the slow cooker, along with the tomatoes, chicken stock, heavy cream, lemon juice, cumin, pepper, cinnamon, salt, cayenne, garlic, and ginger. Stir to combine. Cover and cook on low for 6 hours.

2. About 30 minutes before serving, discard the ginger. Stir in the yogurt. Season with additional salt and pepper, as needed. Cover and continue cooking until warmed through and the flavors have had a chance to meld.

TIP: You're going to want something to sop up the tasty sauce. I'd recommend preparing some basmati rice to go with.

SERVES 4

PREP
15 MINUTES

COOK
6 TO 8 HOURS ON LOW

¼ cup creamy peanut butter

2 tablespoons red
curry paste

2 tablespoons packed
brown sugar

2 tablespoons fish sauce

½ teaspoon kosher salt,
plus more for seasoning

2 tablespoons freshly
squeezed lime juice

1 (14-ounce) can
coconut milk

½ cup Chicken Stock
(page 30) or low-sodium
if store-bought

1 pound boneless, skinless
chicken thighs

3 garlic cloves, minced

3 cups mixed vegetables,
such as sliced red pepper,
sliced red onion, and
snap peas

¼ cup finely chopped fresh
cilantro, for garnish

THAI RED CURRY CHICKEN

Every bit as comforting, but way less ho-hum than your everyday stew, this popular curry is a hassle-free way to imbue your home with global flavors. Feel free to customize the spice level by adding a little more or a bit less curry paste depending on your level of heat tolerance. Me? I'd go for brow-mopping Thai spice any day. Serve with 3 cups of cooked jasmine or basmati rice.

1. In a medium bowl, whisk together the peanut butter, curry paste, brown sugar, fish sauce, salt, lime juice, coconut milk, and chicken stock until thoroughly combined.

2. Put the chicken and garlic in the slow cooker, then spoon the sauce on top. Cover and cook on low for 6 to 8 hours.

3. During the last hour of cooking, add the vegetables. Cover and continue cooking until the vegetables are crisp-tender. Season with additional salt, as needed. Garnish with the cilantro before serving.

TIP: These days, most grocery stores stock jasmine and basmati rice. If yours does not, go ahead and serve your curry with long-grain white rice. This dish won't suffer one bit.

BUTTER CHICKEN

SERVES 6

PREP
10 MINUTES

COOK
6 HOURS ON LOW

Go to any Indian restaurant and you'll likely find this dish. It's no surprise since it hits all the right notes: lushly creamy, a little bit spicy, and heady enough to fragrance your home for days. What it doesn't usually contain, though, is butter. Instead, it's the creaminess of the dish that gives it its name. To wake up the dish after it's spent time cooking, squirt a little fresh lemon juice on it before serving.

1. Put the chicken in the slow cooker, along with the onion, tomatoes, garlic, ginger, jalapeño, heavy cream, chicken stock, tomato paste, garam masala, cumin, turmeric, cinnamon stick, and salt. Stir to combine, cover, and cook on low for 6 hours.

2. During the last 30 minutes of cooking, add the almonds. Cover and continue cooking until warmed through. Season with additional salt and pepper, as needed. Garnish with the cilantro before serving over the rice.

TIP: You can lighten this dish by replacing the heavy cream with 1 cup of plain yogurt. If you choose to do so, though, add it in 20 minutes before serving, continuing the cooking process only long enough to heat it through.

3 pounds boneless, skinless chicken thighs, cut into ½-inch pieces

1 large onion, sliced

2 large Roma tomatoes, diced

4 garlic cloves, minced

2 tablespoons minced peeled fresh ginger

1 jalapeño pepper, minced

1½ cups heavy (whipping) cream

1 cup Chicken Stock (page 30) or low-sodium if store-bought

1½ teaspoons tomato paste

2 teaspoons garam masala

1 teaspoon ground cumin

1 teaspoon ground turmeric

1 cinnamon stick

1 teaspoon kosher salt, plus more for seasoning

3 tablespoons finely chopped almonds

Freshly ground black pepper

¼ cup finely chopped fresh cilantro, for garnish

3 cups cooked white rice, for serving

SERVES 6

PREP
10 MINUTES

COOK
8 HOURS ON LOW

1½ pounds boneless, skinless chicken thighs

2 pounds tomatillos, husked, cleaned, and puréed

1 medium onion, finely chopped

3 garlic cloves, minced

½ cup finely chopped fresh cilantro

2½ cups Chicken Stock (page 30) or low-sodium if store-bought

1 tablespoon chili powder, preferably ancho

1 teaspoon ground cumin

1 teaspoon kosher salt, plus more for seasoning

1 (14.5-ounce) can cannellini or pinto beans, drained and rinsed

Freshly ground black pepper

1 cup crushed tortilla chips, for garnish

½ cup sour cream, for garnish

1 medium red onion, finely chopped, for garnish

1 lime, cut into wedges, for garnish

CHICKEN CHILI VERDE

A welcome alternative to red-sauced chili, this version benefits from the bright flavor of cilantro and puréed tomatillos. If you have a well-stocked Latin market nearby, look for canned tomatillos on the shelf near the chipotle chiles en adobo. They're a worthwhile substitute to fresh tomatillos and save you the work of peeling the husks.

1. Put the chicken in the slow cooker, along with the puréed tomatillos, onion, garlic, cilantro, chicken stock, chili powder, cumin, salt, and beans. Stir to combine. Cover and cook on low for 8 hours.

2. Use two forks to shred the chicken. Season with additional salt and pepper, as needed. Ladle into the bowls and garnish with the tortilla chips, sour cream, red onion, and a squirt of lime.

TIP: In a pinch, you can replace the tomatillos, onion, and cilantro with 1½ cups jarred salsa verde. But be careful not to oversalt, as you can always add more.

CAROLINA BARBECUE CHICKEN

SERVES 4

PREP
15 MINUTES

COOK
6 TO 8 HOURS ON LOW

When it comes to flavor and texture, nothing compares to a grilled bird. But if for whatever reason the grill isn't an option, make use of the two-part process spelled out in this recipe. First the slow cooker develops the flavors and then the broiler crisps up the chicken skin, yielding pretty delicious results. Use homemade barbecue sauce as the basis for this favorite picnic dish. Go ahead and customize the sauce to your liking, adding a bit more vinegar for tang or some hot sauce for a blast of heat.

2½ cups Barbecue Sauce (page 46) or store-bought

¼ cup distilled white vinegar

¼ cup packed brown sugar

1 teaspoon garlic powder

2 pounds chicken drumsticks and thighs

1. In a medium bowl, whisk together the barbecue sauce, vinegar, brown sugar, and garlic powder. Put the chicken in the slow cooker and pour the sauce on top. Cover and cook on low for 6 to 8 hours.

2. Preheat the broiler. Transfer the chicken to an aluminum foil–lined baking sheet. When the oven is hot, place the chicken under the broiler and let it caramelize for 3 to 5 minutes, until the skin starts to crisp and char a bit. Remove from the oven and serve with your favorite sides.

TIP: You can substitute chicken breasts for the drumsticks and thighs. Reduce the cooking time to 4 hours to accommodate the use of white meat, which would dry out during a longer cook time.

SERVES 6

PREP
15 MINUTES

COOK
6 TO 8 HOURS ON LOW
FINAL 30 MINUTES
ON HIGH

1 tablespoon extra-virgin olive oil

3½ pounds bone-in, skin-on chicken thighs

Kosher salt

Freshly ground black pepper

1 teaspoon peppercorns

½ cup soy sauce

½ cup distilled white vinegar

8 garlic cloves, smashed

3 bay leaves

CHICKEN ADOBO

I first had this Filipino dish when my boyfriend's mom sent him home with a batch. It deserves to be on regular rotation in your kitchen—like it is in mine. Do your mealtime up right with a starter of *lumpia* (pork-filled, Shanghai-style egg rolls), with sweet chili sauce for dipping alongside. Then serve the chicken on a bed of rice.

BROWN: In a slow cooker with a stove-top function, or in a Dutch oven or heavy-bottomed pan over medium-high heat, heat the oil until shimmering. Season the chicken with the salt and ground pepper, and brown, about 3 minutes per side.

1. Put the chicken in the slow cooker, along with the peppercorns, soy sauce, vinegar, garlic, and bay leaves. Cover and cook on low for 6 to 8 hours.

2. About 30 minutes before serving, vent the lid of the slow cooker, raise the setting to high, and continue to simmer to allow the sauce to thicken slightly.

3. Meanwhile, preheat the broiler. Transfer the chicken, skin-side up, to an aluminum foil–lined baking sheet. When the oven is hot, place the chicken under the broiler and let the skin crisp for 3 to 5 minutes.

4. Discard the bay leaves. Serve the chicken, spooning the sauce on top.

TIP: For a more flavorful, authentic dish, use palm vinegar in place of white vinegar; you'll find it in Filipino and some Asian markets. Then, mix all of the ingredients together in a resealable bag or container. Transfer them to the refrigerator to marinate overnight. When you're ready, add the marinade to the slow cooker and cook as directed.

Cooking spray or
1 tablespoon extra-virgin
olive oil

1 medium onion, chopped

2 tablespoons minced garlic
(about 6 cloves)

1 green bell pepper, seeded
and roughly chopped

1 red bell pepper, seeded
and roughly chopped

1 pound boneless, skinless
chicken thighs, cut into
½-inch cubes

¼ cup Chicken Stock
(page 30) or low-sodium
if store-bought

3 tablespoons packed
brown sugar

3 tablespoons rice vinegar

½ teaspoon kosher salt,
plus more for seasoning

½ teaspoon ground
white pepper, plus more
for seasoning

1 (8-ounce) can pineapple
chunks, drained

4 teaspoons
cornstarch, mixed with
4 teaspoons water

SWEET AND SOUR CHICKEN

Save money and time and get your takeout fix at home—and have it waiting for you when you open the door. Pair it with egg rolls and use the sweet and sour sauce on your plate as the dip. Really, why not? Serve with white rice.

1. Use the cooking spray or olive oil to coat the inside (bottom and sides) of the slow cooker. Add the onion, garlic, bell peppers, chicken, chicken stock, brown sugar, vinegar, salt, and pepper. Stir to combine. Cover and cook on low for 6 to 8 hours.

2. About 30 minutes before serving, stir together the pineapple and cornstarch in a medium bowl until well combined. Add the mixture to the slow cooker, stir to combine, cover, and continue cooking until the sauce begins to thicken.

3. Season with additional salt and pepper, as needed.

TIP: Go ahead and use fresh pineapple chunks if you prefer. Your dish will taste all the better for it.

CHICKEN TINGA TACOS

SERVES 4

PREP
10 MINUTES

COOK
6 HOURS ON LOW

Slowly poaching chicken thighs in chipotle-spiked, chorizo-stippled red sauce infuses the meat with smoky heat. If there's any leftover meat, serve it the next day for lunch, tucking it into a cheesy quesadilla or using it to top nachos.

1. Season the chicken with the salt. Put the chicken in the slow cooker, along with the chorizo, tomatoes, salsa, chipotle chiles and sauce, and vinegar and stir to combine. Cover and cook on low for 6 hours, until tender.

2. Remove the cover. Use two forks to shred the meat and mix with the sauce to coat. Season with additional salt, as needed.

3. Serve the mixture in the warm tortillas with the avocado, red onion, and cilantro.

TIP: You can substitute boneless, skinless chicken breasts for the chicken thighs. If you do, reduce the cooking time to 4 hours. Otherwise, the meat will dry out.

2 pounds boneless, skinless chicken thighs

1 teaspoon kosher salt, plus more for seasoning

2 ounces Mexican chorizo, casing removed

2 (14.5-ounce) can diced, fire-roasted tomatoes, undrained

2 cups store-bought salsa

2 or 3 chipotle chiles en adobo, finely chopped, plus 1 tablespoon adobo sauce

1 tablespoon apple cider vinegar

10 to 12 tortillas, warm, for serving

2 avocados, peeled, pitted, and diced

¼ cup chopped red onion

¼ cup chopped fresh cilantro

SERVES 6

PREP
15 MINUTES

COOK
6 TO 8 HOURS ON LOW

3½ pounds chicken drumsticks and thighs, skinned

4 medium carrots, cut into matchsticks (about 2 cups)

1 small onion, diced

2 garlic cloves, minced

1½ cups Chicken Stock (page 30) or low-sodium if store-bought

½ cup dry white wine, such as Pinot Grigio

¼ cup heavy (whipping) cream

1 teaspoon poultry seasoning

½ teaspoon kosher salt, plus more for seasoning

½ teaspoon freshly ground black pepper

2 tablespoons all-purpose flour

2 tablespoons freshly squeezed lemon juice

3 tablespoons chopped fresh tarragon leaves, for garnish

CHICKEN FRICASSEE

The basic ingredients of this comforting French dish are simple—chicken simmered in wine with a little cream, a few vegetables, and a sprinkling of spices. From there, chicken fricassee has undergone countless variations. Serve this version with mashed potatoes, creamy grits, or a garlic-infused polenta.

1. Put the chicken in the slow cooker, along with the carrots, onion, garlic, chicken stock, wine, heavy cream, poultry seasoning, salt, and pepper. Stir to combine. Cover and cook on low for 6 to 8 hours.

2. About 30 minutes before serving, spoon out ¼ cup of cooking liquid from the slow cooker and whisk it in a small bowl with the flour, taking care that no lumps remain. Pour the mixture back into the slow cooker, add the lemon juice, and whisk to combine. Cover and continue cooking until the sauce is slightly thickened.

3. Season with additional salt, as needed. Serve, garnished with the tarragon, alongside your favorite starch.

TIP: A crisp, lightly dressed green salad is an ideal accompaniment to this dish, as it cuts through the richness of the sauce.

TURKEY TETRAZZINI

SERVES 4

PREP
10 MINUTES

COOK
6 HOURS ON LOW

The first time I had this dish—I mean, really had this dish—was from a pizza place in my old neighborhood. Fresh out of college and hungry for something other than ramen, it satisfied my cravings and then some. The secret ingredient is dry sherry, which makes a world of difference. Typically, I include sautéed mushrooms; however, they don't always lend themselves to the slow cooking process. If you want them in your dish, sauté them in a pan and add them right before serving, instead. Serve this dish on spaghetti or linguine.

Cooking spray or 1 tablespoon extra-virgin olive oil

3 cups diced cooked turkey

1 small onion, finely chopped

2 cups Chicken Stock (page 30) or low-sodium if store-bought

1 cup heavy (whipping) cream

2 tablespoons dry sherry

1½ cups grated Parmesan cheese, plus more for garnish

4 ounces cream cheese

1 teaspoon kosher salt, plus more for seasoning

½ teaspoon freshly ground black pepper, plus more for seasoning

⅛ teaspoon ground nutmeg

1 cup frozen peas

1. Use the cooking spray or olive oil to coat the inside (bottom and sides) of the slow cooker. Add the turkey, onion, chicken stock, heavy cream, sherry, Parmesan, cream cheese, salt, pepper, and nutmeg. Stir to combine. Cover and cook on low for 6 hours.

2. About 25 minutes before serving, add the peas. Season with additional salt and pepper, as needed. When the peas have finished cooking, serve and garnish with extra grated Parmesan.

TIP: For the best results, take an extra step and sauté the mushrooms in butter on the stove top and add them in to your dish right before serving. It'll prevent them from getting rubbery, as they tend to become in the slow cooker.

HEARTY TURKEY CHILI

SERVES 6

PREP
15 MINUTES

COOK
8 HOURS ON LOW

There's no shame in wanting a break from beef, and turkey chili is just the thing. It's still hearty, but it's lighter and lower in calories. Just be sure to season it generously, or your chili will be bland. For a bit more depth of flavor, add 1½ teaspoons of unsweetened cocoa powder; it makes all the difference, but if you hadn't put it in yourself, you'd never know it's there.

BROWN: In a slow cooker with a stove-top function, or in a Dutch oven or heavy-bottomed pan over medium-high heat, heat the oil until shimmering. Add the turkey and brown, breaking it up into bits until it is cooked through and no pink remains.

1. Put the turkey in the slow cooker, along with the onions, celery, jalapeños, bell pepper, garlic, chili beans and liquid, diced tomatoes, tomato paste, chili powder, cumin, salt, oregano, and bay leaves. Stir to combine, then cover and cook for 8 hours.

2. Season with additional salt, as needed. Ladle the chili into bowls and serve with the cheese, sour cream, cilantro or chives, and limes.

TIP: Make the chili ahead and let it sit in the refrigerator overnight—its flavors will deepen.

1 tablespoon extra-virgin olive oil

2 pounds ground turkey

2 medium onions, finely chopped

2 celery stalks, finely chopped

2 jalapeño peppers, finely chopped

1 red bell pepper, seeded and finely chopped

3 garlic cloves, minced

2 (15-ounce) cans chili beans, undrained

2 (15.5-ounce) cans diced tomatoes, preferably fire-roasted, undrained

2 tablespoons tomato paste

3 tablespoons chili powder

2 teaspoons ground cumin

1 teaspoon kosher salt, plus more for seasoning

1 teaspoon dried oregano

2 bay leaves

2 cups shredded sharp Cheddar cheese, for garnish

1 cup sour cream, for garnish

¼ cup chopped fresh cilantro or chives, for garnish

1 lime, cut into wedges, for garnish

NEW ENGLAND–STYLE CLAM CHOWDER (PAGE 147)

7

FISH & SEAFOOD

THERE'S SOMETHING COUNTER-

intuitive about making fish and seafood in the slow cooker—it cooks quickly, after all. And it just cannot be left cooking, even at a low temperature, for hours on end. However, I suggest you don't rule it out. With the proper base or poaching liquid, the low-and-slow approach works "swimmingly," yielding sweet and flavorful tender results. Just be sure to save these recipes for the weekend, or whenever you're around the house, as the seafood needs to be added toward the end of cooking.

1 pound waxy baby potatoes, such as Yukon Gold

2 medium onions, finely chopped

2 celery stalks, finely chopped

5 garlic cloves, minced

1 (28-ounce) can crushed tomatoes

1 (8-ounce) bottle clam juice

8 ounces Fish Stock (page 31) or low-sodium if store-bought

1 (6-ounce) can tomato paste

1 tablespoon balsamic vinegar

1 teaspoon sugar

½ teaspoon celery salt

½ teaspoon kosher salt, plus more for seasoning

½ teaspoon freshly ground black pepper, plus more for seasoning

2 bay leaves

1 pound firm-fleshed white fish, such as cod, cut into 1-inch pieces

½ pound medium uncooked shrimp, shelled and deveined

½ pound scallops, small side muscle removed, halved

¼ cup finely chopped flat-leaf parsley, for garnish

SEAFOOD STEW

Light, fragrant, and rich all at once, this seafood stew covers all the bases, offering a little bit of tang and a touch of sugar to pick up on the sweetness of the fish, scallops, and shrimp. Meanwhile, the fact that the vegetable-bolstered broth cooks low and slow gives it the chance to build flavor and complexity.

1. To the slow cooker, add the potatoes, onions, celery, garlic, tomatoes, clam juice, fish stock, tomato paste, vinegar, sugar, celery salt, kosher salt, pepper, and bay leaves. Stir to combine. Cover and cook on low for 6 hours, or until the potatoes are tender when pierced with a fork.

2. About 30 minutes before serving, add the white fish, shrimp, and scallops. Cover and continue cooking on low until cooked through.

3. Discard the bay leaves. Season with additional salt and pepper, as needed. Ladle the stew into bowls, garnish with the parsley, and serve immediately.

TIP: Feel free to use whatever herbs you have handy in your garden, such as basil, tarragon or dill, to finish the stew.

NEW ENGLAND-STYLE CLAM CHOWDER

SERVES 6

PREP
20 MINUTES

COOK
8 HOURS ON LOW

For the most flavor in this dish, you'll want to brown the bacon. Go ahead and use any residual bacon grease, too. After all, chowder is not meant to be light. That's what makes it such a treat. Then, finish it with some fresh herbs, such as finely chopped chives, which lend color and fresh flavor.

BROWN: In a slow cooker with a stove top function, or in a Dutch oven or heavy-bottomed pan over medium-high heat, add the bacon and cook until browned on both sides, about 5 minutes.

1. If browned outside the slow cooker, place the bacon and bacon grease in the slow cooker now. Add the clam juice, potatoes, celery, onion, garlic, salt, and pepper. Stir to combine. Cover and cook on low for 8 hours.

2. During the last 30 minutes of cooking, add the half-and-half, heavy cream, and clams. Cover and continue cooking the chowder until it's warmed through. Take care to not let it boil.

3. Season with additional salt and pepper, as needed. Ladle the chowder into bowls and serve immediately.

TIP: Add a finishing crunch to your chowder with some oyster crackers or croutons.

3 bacon slices, finely chopped

1½ cups clam juice

½ pound waxy potatoes, such as Yukon Gold, chopped

2 celery stalks, finely chopped

1 medium onion, minced

2 garlic cloves, minced

1 teaspoon kosher salt, plus more for seasoning

½ teaspoon freshly ground black pepper, plus more for seasoning

2½ cups half-and-half

1 cup heavy (whipping) cream

2 (10-ounce) cans chopped clams, undrained

SERVES 6

PREP
15 MINUTES

COOK
6 HOURS ON LOW

1 tablespoon extra-virgin olive oil

4 ounces meaty salt pork, rind removed and cut into ⅓-inch dice

2 medium onions, minced

2 bay leaves

6 fresh thyme sprigs

5 cups Fish Stock (page 31) or low-sodium if store-bought

1 teaspoon kosher salt, plus more for seasoning

½ teaspoon freshly ground black pepper, plus more for seasoning

2 medium carrots, peeled and thinly sliced

¼ cup diced red pepper

3 pounds skinless, firm-fleshed white fish, such as cod, cut into 1-inch pieces

1 cup broccoli florets, roughly chopped

2 cups cooked macaroni

SMOKY FISH SOUP WITH VEGETABLES

There is a lot of flavor in this hearty soup. A bowlful offers a bounty of tender, succulent, flaky, and seriously flavorful protein offset by a touch of salt pork–inflected smoke. It will take the nip out of a rainy day. If you want even more flavor, garnish with garlicky croutons.

BROWN: In a slow cooker with a stove-top function, or in a Dutch oven or heavy-bottomed pan over medium-high heat, heat the oil until shimmering. Add the salt pork and brown on all sides, about 5 minutes total.

1. If browned outside the slow cooker, place the salt pork in the slow cooker. Add the onions, bay leaves, thyme, fish stock, salt, and pepper. Stir to combine. Cover and cook on low for 6 hours.

2. About 1 hour before serving, add the carrots and red pepper. Cover and continue cooking.

3. About 30 minutes before serving, add the fish and broccoli. Cover and continue cooking until the fish is flakey and no longer translucent.

4. Discard the bay leaves and thyme sprigs. Season with additional salt and pepper, as needed. Ladle the soup into bowls and serve immediately.

TIP: Although it's not required, a sprinkle of fresh, finely chopped chives is a welcome finishing touch. They lend both oniony flavor and a shock of color. Or, brighten the flavor of the soup by adding a dab of herbaceous pesto to each bowl.

TUNA CASSEROLE

Cooking spray or
1 tablespoon extra-virgin
olive oil

2 cups uncooked,
dry egg noodles

1 medium onion, finely
chopped

½ cup sliced mushrooms

¾ cup Chicken Stock
(page 30) or low-sodium
if store-bought

¾ cup heavy
(whipping) cream

½ teaspoon kosher salt,
plus more for seasoning

½ teaspoon freshly ground
black pepper, plus more
for seasoning

2 (5-ounce) cans tuna
in water, drained

½ cup shredded
Swiss cheese

1 cup frozen peas

To me, tuna casserole is a quintessential "housewife" dish. That makes me want to run for the hills, truth be told. Still, there's something downright nostalgic about this casserole, conjuring memories of childhood suppers, when meals weren't the center of getting from point A to B, but rather a time for the family to come together and share tales about their days.

1. Use the cooking spray or olive oil to coat the inside (bottom and sides) of the slow cooker. Add the noodles, onion, mushrooms, chicken stock, heavy cream, salt, pepper, and tuna. Stir to combine. Cover and cook on low for 4 hours, stirring every hour or so to prevent sticking.

2. During the last 20 minutes of cooking, add the cheese and peas. Cover and continue cooking until the cheese has melted. Season with additional salt and pepper, as needed. Serve immediately.

TIP: Mushrooms really are best sautéed on the stove top and added to the dish toward the end of cooking. Take my advice for the best results.

CIOPPINO

This Italian-American seafood stew originated in San Francisco. Traditionally made with the catch of the day from the Pacific Ocean, it may brim with a mix of clams, Dungeness crab, scallops, shrimp, and squid. Keep it authentic by serving slices of toasted sourdough alongside.

SAUTÉ: In a slow cooker with a stove-top function, or in a Dutch oven or heavy-bottomed pan over medium heat, heat the oil until shimmering. Add the fennel, onion, and garlic and sauté until starting to soften, about 5 minutes. Add the wine, then raise the heat to medium-high to bring to a boil. Simmer for 1 minute.

1. If sautéed outside the slow cooker, or not sautéed at all, add the vegetable mixture to the slow cooker, along with the salt, pepper, red pepper flakes, tomato paste, canned tomatoes, chicken stock, clam juice, and bay leaves. Stir to combine. Cover and cook on low for 6 hours.

2. About 30 minutes before serving, add the mussels, clams, fish, and shrimp. Cover and continue cooking until the fish flakes easily with a fork and the clams and mussels open. (Discard any that have not opened.)

3. Discard the bay leaves. Season with additional salt and pepper, as needed. Ladle into bowls, garnish with the basil, and serve.

TIP: When you buy mussels, immediately unwrap them to let them breathe once you get them home. Throw out any mussel that is chipped, broken, or damaged, and toss any mussel that is open. To remove the beard, hold the mussel in one hand, cover the other hand with a dry towel, and grab the beard, pulling it toward the mussel's hinge. Throw out any "threads."

2 tablespoons extra-virgin olive oil

1 fennel bulb, thinly sliced

1 medium onion, finely chopped

4 garlic cloves, minced

1½ cups dry white wine

1¼ teaspoons kosher salt, plus more for seasoning

½ teaspoon freshly ground black pepper, plus more for seasoning

¼ teaspoon red pepper flakes

2 tablespoons tomato paste

1 (28-ounce) can diced tomatoes, preferably fire-roasted, undrained

1 cup Chicken Stock (page 30) or low-sodium if store-bought

1 cup clam juice

2 bay leaves

1 pound mussels, scrubbed and debearded

1 pound Manila clams, scrubbed

1 pound firm-fleshed white fish, such as cod, cut into 1-inch pieces

1 pound large shrimp, peeled and deveined

¼ cup chopped fresh basil

2 large onions,
finely chopped

2 celery stalks,
finely chopped

1 green bell pepper, seeded
and finely chopped

4 garlic cloves, minced

1 (28-ounce) can diced
tomatoes, undrained

1 tablespoon
Worcestershire sauce

1 tablespoon hot sauce,
such as Tabasco

1 teaspoon kosher salt,
plus more for seasoning

½ teaspoon freshly ground
black pepper, plus more
for seasoning

½ teaspoon cayenne pepper

½ teaspoon Cajun or
Creole seasoning

2 bay leaves

1½ pounds large shrimp,
shelled and deveined

4 scallions, sliced,
for garnish

SHRIMP CREOLE

This down-South dish capitalizes on Louisiana's access to fresh, sweet Gulf shrimp. The spiciness of the tomato sauce is tempered by the steaming white rice beneath. You can adjust the heat level by adding or subtracting the amount of Cajun seasoning, hot sauce, and cayenne.

1. To the slow cooker, add the onions, celery, bell pepper, garlic, tomatoes, Worcestershire sauce, hot sauce, salt, pepper, cayenne, Cajun seasoning, and bay leaves. Stir to combine. Cover and cook on low for 6 hours.

2. About 25 minutes before serving, add the shrimp. Cover and continue cooking until the shrimp are pink and no longer translucent.

3. Discard the bay leaves. Season with additional salt and pepper, as needed. Serve with rice and garnish with the scallions.

TIP: Take care not to overcook the shrimp. They're finished when they turn pink and curl up.

SERVES 4

PREP
15 MINUTES

COOK
30 MINUTES ON HIGH,
45 MINUTES ON LOW

2 cups water

1 cup dry white wine

1 lemon, thinly sliced

2 tablespoons minced onion

2 garlic cloves, thinly sliced

3 fresh thyme sprigs

3 fresh tarragon sprigs

1 teaspoon peppercorns

2 pounds skin-on salmon
or 4 skin-on fillets

1 teaspoon kosher salt,
plus more for seasoning

1 cup sour cream

¾ cup mayonnaise

2 tablespoons chopped
fresh chives

2 tablespoons chopped
fresh dill

2 tablespoons freshly
squeezed lemon juice

Freshly ground black pepper

Extra-virgin olive oil,
for garnish

Lemon wedges, for garnish

LEMONY SALMON
WITH FRESH HERBS AND DILL CREAM

Salmon, lemon, and dill—they're a perfect culinary trio. And, as it turns out, the slow cooker is the perfect way to indulge. Poached in citrus-spiked white wine and herbs, the fish cooks just until flaky and is finished with a whirl of olive oil, sprinkle of salt, and more lemon. But the pièce de résistance is the creamy, dill-flecked sauce that goes with it.

1. To the slow cooker, add the water, wine, lemon, onion, garlic, thyme, tarragon, and peppercorns. Stir to combine. Cover and cook on high for 30 minutes.

2. Season the salmon with the salt and place it in the slow cooker. Reduce the heat to low. Cover and cook for 45 minutes or until the fish flakes easily and is no longer opaque.

3. While the salmon is cooking, combine the sour cream, mayonnaise, chives, dill, and lemon juice in a medium bowl. Season with additional salt and pepper, as needed. Stir to combine, and set aside.

4. Remove the salmon from the poaching liquid and discard the liquid. Serve the salmon drizzled with olive oil, a sprinkle of coarse salt, lemon wedges, and the reserved dill cream sauce.

TIP: The salmon can be held on the warm setting for up to 1 hour before serving.

SEAFOOD POT-AU-FEU

SERVES 6

PREP
10 MINUTES

COOK
6 HOURS ON LOW

Traditionally made with beef, this lighter take on the quintessential French stew is super-flexible in terms of ingredients, meaning you can substitute whatever seafood and root vegetables you like. Even the spices and herbs can suit your taste. Add a few cloves or a dash of nutmeg, or toss in some turnips and cabbage. Mustard and horseradish are welcome accompaniments in my house.

1. To the slow cooker, add the leek, fennel, carrots, onion, garlic, fish stock, wine, tomatoes, salt, pepper, red pepper flakes, bay leaf, and turmeric. Stir to combine. Cover and cook on low for 6 hours.

2. About 45 minutes before serving, add the white fish, salmon, mussels, and shrimp. Cover and cook until the fish flakes easily and is opaque, and the mussels have all opened. Discard the bay leaf, along with any mussels that have not opened. Season with additional salt and pepper, as needed.

3. Ladle the soup into bowls, garnish with the chopped herbs, such as thyme, parsley, and tarragon, and serve immediately.

TIP: This soup all but demands a crusty baguette. Pick one up, and use it to sop up the savory broth.

1 small leek (white and light green parts), thinly sliced and washed

1 small fennel bulb, trimmed and thinly sliced

12 baby carrots

1 medium onion, finely chopped

2 garlic cloves, thinly sliced

7 cups Fish Stock (page 31) or low-sodium if store-bought

¼ cup dry white wine

1 (15-ounce) can diced tomatoes, undrained

¾ teaspoon kosher salt, plus more for seasoning

½ teaspoon freshly ground black pepper, plus more for seasoning

¼ teaspoon red pepper flakes

1 bay leaf

⅛ teaspoon ground turmeric

¾ pound boneless, skinless, firm-fleshed white fish, such as cod, cut into 1-inch cubes

½ pound boneless, skinless salmon, cut into 1-inch cubes

12 small mussels, scrubbed and debearded

½ pound medium shrimp, shelled and deveined

¼ cup mixed chopped fresh herbs, for garnish

8 medium red potatoes

2 large, sweet onions, such as Vidalia, quartered

2 pounds smoked sausage, cut into 3-inch pieces

1 (3-ounce) package seafood boil seasoning

1 (12-ounce) bottle pale ale beer

10 cups water

4 ears of corn, halved

2 pounds medium raw shrimp, shelled and deveined

Cocktail sauce, for serving

Hot sauce, for serving

½ cup melted butter, for serving

1 large lemon, cut into wedges, for garnish

LOW COUNTRY SEAFOOD BOIL

Seafood boils are one of the great pleasures of summer in many places throughout the country. In the Midwest, where I live, there's the Door County fish boil. The East Coast affords Old Bay–spiked crab boils, while New England clambakes often take place on the beach. In this book, the Low Country approach provides every bit of a finger-licking social gathering. If you've never participated in a seafood boil, now's your chance. Invite some friends and have some Wet-Naps handy and ice-cold beers ready—you'll need them. If you can't find a package of seafood boil seasoning at your grocery store, it can easily be purchased online.

1. In the slow cooker, put the potatoes, onions, smoked sausage, seafood boil seasoning, beer, and water. Stir to combine. Cover and cook for 6 hours, or until the potatoes are tender when pierced with a fork.

2. About 45 minutes before serving, add the corn. Cover and continue cooking for 25 minutes. Add the shrimp, cover, and continue cooking until the shrimp are pink and no longer translucent.

3. Drain the slow cooker, discard the cooking liquid, and serve the seafood with cocktail sauce, hot sauce, melted butter, and lemon wedges.

TIP: When serving a crowd, I like to line an outdoor table with newspaper and pour the drained contents on top, letting everyone grab the items they crave, while chatting in communal fashion.

WHITE BEANS
WITH TUNA AND TOMATOES

SERVES 6

PREP
10 MINUTES

COOK
8 TO 10 HOURS
ON LOW

Humble beans make a hearty, affordable base for this one-pot tuna dish, while pepperoncini and cherry tomatoes make it truly pop. I much prefer tuna packed in oil, but using it here makes the dish greasy. So, you're better off going with water-packed.

1. To the slow cooker, add the beans, onion, garlic, bay leaves, salt, pepper, Italian seasoning, and 6 cups of chicken stock. Stir to combine, cover, and cook on low for 8 to 10 hours, adding additional stock as needed.

2. About 30 minutes before serving, add the tomatoes, pepperoncini, and tuna. Stir to combine. Cover and continue cooking until warmed through and the beans are tender when pierced with a fork.

3. Discard the bay leaves. Season with additional salt and pepper, as needed. Spoon into bowls and serve immediately.

TIP: There is no exact rule of thumb when it comes to cooking beans in the slow cooker. Cooking time varies by variety, vessel, and the age of the beans. The first time you try, it's wise to stay nearby.

1 pound small white beans, such as cannellini, soaked overnight, drained, and rinsed

1 medium onion, finely chopped

2 garlic cloves, minced

2 bay leaves

1¼ teaspoons kosher salt, plus more for seasoning

½ teaspoon freshly ground black pepper, plus more for seasoning

½ teaspoon Italian seasoning

6 to 8 cups Chicken Stock (page 30) or low-sodium if store-bought

1 pound cherry tomatoes

2 tablespoons pepperoncini, chopped

2 (5-ounce) cans tuna in water, drained

ARTICHOKE-PARMESAN DIP WITH CROSTINI (PAGE 171)

8

VEGETABLES, SIDES & DIPS

NO ONE CAN LIVE ON MEAT AND meat alone. Fortunately, the slow cooker is a versatile vessel that turns out stellar veggies, sides, and dips that just happen to pair especially well with meaty dishes. They may play a supporting role in this cookbook, but I think you'll find they're worthy of your slow cooker's time. Whether you're looking to maximize oven space during the holidays, bring appetizers to a party, or have something to round out the main meal, you'll find plenty of delicious, comforting, and fun recipes to choose from.

12 ears of corn, shucked
and cut from the cob,
or 2 pounds frozen
corn kernels

2 bacon slices,
finely chopped

8 ounces cream cheese,
at room temperature

6 ounces American cheese,
finely diced

½ cup whole milk

3 ounces sour cream

3 fresh thyme sprigs

2 bay leaves

¾ teaspoon kosher salt,
plus more for seasoning

½ teaspoon freshly ground
black pepper, plus more
for seasoning

CHEESY CREAMED CORN
WITH BACON

This creamy, tangy corn is a steakhouse-inspired
side dish that goes well with grilled or roasted meat.
While a stove-top version would require an attentive
eye, the slow cooker takes the work out of the dish,
demanding only an occasional stir.

1. In the slow cooker, combine the corn, bacon, cream cheese,
cheese, milk, sour cream, thyme, and bay leaves. Season with
the salt and pepper, and stir to combine. Cover and cook on
low for 3 hours, until the corn is cooked and the sauce has
thickened slightly.

2. Remove the cover and discard the thyme and bay leaves. Season with additional salt and pepper as needed, and serve.

TIP: Nothing beats the taste of fresh, shucked sweet corn. If it's
not in season, use frozen kernels instead, and reduce the cooking
time by 1 hour.

CORN PUDDING
WITH POBLANOS

SERVES 8

PREP
5 MINUTES

COOK
3 TO 4 HOURS ON LOW

Corn muffins and cornbread are classic companions to chili and barbecue fare. This slow cooker variation also goes well with all kinds of south of the border fare, thanks to the addition of poblanos. For a real treat, drizzle it with a little honey before serving, or serve whipped honey butter alongside.

1. Use the cooking spray or olive oil to coat the inside (bottom and sides) of the slow cooker. To the slow cooker add the cream cheese, corn, peppers, muffin mix, milk, sugar, eggs, and salt. Stir to combine. Cover and cook on low for 3 to 4 hours or until a knife inserted into the center of the pudding comes out clean.

2. Let stand for 5 minutes before serving.

TIP: You can make this pudding cheesy by mixing in 1½ cups of shredded Cheddar or pepper Jack cheese.

Cooking spray or
1 tablespoon extra-virgin
olive oil

1 (8-ounce) package
cream cheese, at room
temperature

2 cups fresh corn, removed
from the cob

2 poblano peppers, seeded,
stemmed, and finely diced

1 (8.5-ounce) package corn
muffin mix

1 cup whole milk

⅓ cup sugar

2 eggs, beaten

1 teaspoon kosher salt

Cooking spray or
1 tablespoon extra-virgin
olive oil

3 pounds beets, scrubbed,
peeled, and cut into wedges

2 garlic cloves, minced

1 cup white grape or
apple juice

½ cup balsamic vinegar

1 tablespoon honey

2 fresh thyme sprigs

1 teaspoon kosher salt,
plus more for seasoning

½ teaspoon freshly ground
black pepper, plus more
for seasoning

1 tablespoon cold water

1 tablespoon cornstarch

BALSAMIC BEETS

Canned beets gave fresh beets a bad name. If you're averse, I'd like to suggest giving them another chance. These tangy balsamic beets bear little resemblance to the cloying ones many of us avoid. Instead, they capitalize on the inherent sweetness and lovely color of beets, while veering in a savory direction. Elevate them further by finishing the beets with toasted walnuts and dollops of herbed goat cheese.

1. Use the cooking spray or olive oil to coat the inside (bottom and sides) of the slow cooker. Add the beets, garlic, juice, vinegar, honey, thyme, salt, and pepper. Stir to combine. Cover and cook on high for 3 to 4 hours.

2. About 10 minutes before serving, combine the water and cornstarch in a small bowl, stirring until no lumps remain. Add to the slow cooker and continue to cook for 10 minutes, or until the sauce thickens.

3. Discard the thyme. Season with additional salt and pepper, as needed. Serve.

TIP: Go ahead and use whatever herbs you have on hand to finish the beets. Parsley, chives, and basil work particularly well.

HASH BROWN CASEROLE

SERVES 8

PREP
10 MINUTES

COOK
1½ HOURS ON HIGH,
THEN 2½ HOURS ON LOW

This slow cooker version of the popular potato side dish works as well for brunch as it does for dinner. It's equally delicious alongside Ham with Root Vegetables (page 85) as it is with Easter Lamb (page 107). One thing to watch for as it cooks is the moisture level. If the casserole starts looking a little dry, adding a small amount of stock should set it right.

1. Use the cooking spray or olive oil to coat the inside (bottom and sides) of the slow cooker. In a large bowl, combine the onion, garlic, hash browns, Cheddar, sour cream, chicken stock, heavy cream, salt, pepper, and onion powder. Stir until thoroughly mixed. Add the mixture to the slow cooker. Cover and cook on high for 1½ hours. Reduce the heat to low and cook for another 2½ hours.

2. Season with additional salt, if needed. Let the casserole sit for 10 minutes before serving.

TIP: You can make this dish using freshly shredded potatoes. If you do, though, wrap them in a kitchen towel and squeeze out all the moisture prior to incorporating them.

Cooking spray or 1 tablespoon extra-virgin olive oil

1 medium onion, finely chopped

3 garlic cloves, minced

1 (32-ounce bag) frozen hash brown potatoes, thawed

3 cups shredded sharp Cheddar cheese

2 cups sour cream

1¼ cups Chicken Stock (page 30) or low-sodium if store-bought

½ cup heavy (whipping) cream

¾ teaspoon kosher salt, plus more for seasoning

½ teaspoon freshly ground black pepper

½ teaspoon onion powder

½ pound bacon, diced

2 garlic cloves, minced

3 pounds waxy potatoes, such as Yukon Gold, peeled and diced

1 (8-ounce) package cream cheese, at room temperature

1 cup sour cream

½ cup butter, cut into chunks, at room temperature

½ cup Chicken Stock (page 30) or low-sodium if store-bought

¼ cup heavy (whipping) cream

3 cups shredded sharp Cheddar cheese

4 scallions, thinly sliced

1 teaspoon kosher salt, plus more for seasoning

½ teaspoon freshly ground black pepper, plus more for seasoning

½ teaspoon garlic powder

½ teaspoon onion powder

LOADED MASHED POTATOES

Seriously, who doesn't love mashed potatoes, much less ones loaded with bacon, sour cream, and cheese. You get all that and more in this slow cooker rendition, and any leftovers can easily be turned into potato cakes. Best of all, it goes with most everything, including Mississippi Beef Roast (page 66) and Red Wine–Braised Lamb Shoulder (page 112).

BROWN: In a slow cooker with a stove-top function, or in a Dutch oven or heavy-bottomed pan over medium-high heat, add the bacon and cook until browned, about 5 minutes. Add the garlic, then reduce the heat to medium and continue cooking 1 minute more.

1. If browned outside the slow cooker, place the bacon mixture in the slow cooker. Add the potatoes, cream cheese, sour cream, butter, chicken stock, heavy cream, Cheddar, scallions, salt, pepper, garlic powder, and onion powder. Stir to combine. Cover and cook on low for 3 hours.

2. Let the potato mixture sit for 10 minutes. Season with additional salt and pepper, as needed, and serve.

TIP: Make cleanup easy by using a slow cooker liner for this dish.

SAUSAGE AND APPLE STUFFING

SERVES 8

PREP
15 MINUTES

COOK
3 HOURS ON LOW

I can't make stuffing without thinking of my favorite holiday, Thanksgiving. An adaptation of the side dish I prepare each year, this sausage and apple stuffing fills my home with a happiness-inducing scent. I think—I hope—it'll do the same for you.

BROWN: In a slow cooker with a stove-top function, or in a Dutch oven or heavy-bottomed pan over medium-high heat, heat 1 tablespoon of olive oil until shimmering. Add the sausage and brown, breaking it up into small bits until no pink remains. Add the celery, onion, apple, and garlic and continue cooking, stirring occasionally, for another 5 minutes.

1. Use the cooking spray or the remaining 1 tablespoon of olive oil to coat the inside (bottom and sides) of the slow cooker. If browned outside the slow cooker, add the sausage mixture to the slow cooker. Add the bread, sage, thyme, chicken stock, butter, salt, and pepper. Stir to combine. Cover and cook on low for 3 hours.

2. Season with additional salt and pepper, as needed. Let the stuffing sit for 10 minutes before serving.

TIP: Use leftovers as a stuffing for split chicken breasts. Put the stuffing into split chicken breasts, then wrap and tie with kitchen twine or spear with toothpicks to seal. Bake in a 350°F oven for 45 minutes or until the chicken is no longer pink. Top with Swiss cheese and put it back in the oven until the cheese turns golden and bubbly. (Be sure to discard the twine or toothpicks before serving.)

Cooking spray or
2 tablespoons extra-virgin
olive oil, divided

½ pound bulk sausage

2 celery stalks,
finely chopped

1 large onion, finely chipped

1 large tart apple, cored
and chopped

2 garlic cloves, minced

7 cups cubed crusty French
bread, stale

1½ teaspoons dried sage

½ teaspoon dried thyme

1⅔ cups Chicken Stock
(page 30) or low-sodium
if store-bought

2 tablespoons unsalted
butter, melted

½ teaspoon kosher salt,
plus more for seasoning

¼ teaspoon freshly ground
black pepper, plus more
for seasoning

Cooking spray or
1 tablespoon extra-virgin
olive oil

2 pounds baby carrots

2 tablespoons
butter, melted

3 sprigs fresh thyme

½ cup packed brown sugar

⅓ cup balsamic vinegar

½ teaspoon kosher salt

¼ teaspoon freshly ground
black pepper

⅛ teaspoon
ground cinnamon

TANGY-SWEET GLAZED CARROTS

Carrots are one of my favorite veggies—not only because they're sweet, but also because they're a great vehicle for other flavors. Here, they get a boost from balsamic vinegar, while a touch of brown sugar works magic. The end result is something caramelized and piquant—just what you want next to Ham and Scalloped Potatoes (page 84).

1. Use the cooking spray or olive oil to coat the inside (bottom and sides) of the slow cooker. Add the carrots, butter, and thyme to the slow cooker. Stir to combine. Cover and cook on low for 3 to 4 hours, or until tender. Discard the thyme sprigs.

2. Meanwhile, mix together the brown sugar, vinegar, salt, pepper, and cinnamon. Add the mixture to the slow cooker and toss with the carrots before serving.

TIP: For a more refined look, instead use 2 pounds of scrubbed, peeled rainbow carrots or orange carrots with the stems intact.

SERVES 6

PREP
10 MINUTES

COOK
6 TO 8 HOURS ON LOW

Cooking spray or
1 tablespoon extra-virgin
olive oil

1 pound dried navy beans,
picked over, soaked
overnight, drained,
and rinsed

8 thick-cut bacon slices,
finely diced

1 medium onion, minced

2 garlic cloves, minced

2½ cups water

½ cup ketchup

¼ cup molasses

¼ cup maple syrup

¼ cup packed brown sugar

2 tablespoons cider vinegar

1 tablespoon
prepared mustard

1¼ teaspoons kosher salt,
plus more for seasoning

½ teaspoon freshly ground
black pepper, plus more
for seasoning

SMOKY BAKED BEANS

Beans are a beloved side dish across many cultures, appearing on tables from Ireland and the United Kingdom to Boston, where they're traditionally made with molasses or maple syrup and salt pork or bacon. Channeling the latter, these baked beans are the perfect side dish to Carolina Barbecue Chicken (page 135) or Barbecue Pulled Pork (page 77). Plus, they're an easy way to feed a crowd.

1. Use the cooking spray or olive oil to coat the inside (bottom and sides) of the slow cooker. Add the beans, bacon, onion, garlic, water, ketchup, molasses, maple syrup, brown sugar, vinegar, mustard, salt, and pepper. Stir to combine. Cover and cook on low for 6 to 8 hours, or until the beans are tender when pierced with a fork.

2. Season with additional salt and pepper, as needed. Serve.

TIP: The beans can be frozen in an airtight container for up to 1 month. Thaw the beans in the refrigerator before reheating over low heat.

Cooking spray or
1 tablespoon extra-virgin
olive oil

3 pounds collard greens,
washed, stemmed and
leaves torn

1 leftover ham bone
(page 85)

1 large onion, minced

3 garlic cloves, minced

2 cups Chicken Stock
(page 30) or low-sodium
if store-bought

1¼ tablespoons
balsamic vinegar

1 tablespoon packed
dark brown sugar

1¼ teaspoons kosher salt,
plus more for seasoning

½ teaspoon freshly ground
black pepper, plus more
for seasoning

½ teaspoon red
pepper flakes

TANGY COLLARD GREENS

Thick, bitter collards—thought to date back to ancient Greece—are high in vitamins A, K, and C. And they're a staple in Southern cuisine. For variety, mix them with kale, turnip greens, and mustard greens, and give them plenty of time to mellow out, knowing that the brown sugar, smoky ham, and chicken stock help lend balance to this soul-food standby.

1. Use the cooking spray or olive oil to coat the inside (bottom and sides) of the slow cooker. In the slow cooker put the greens, ham bone, onion, garlic, chicken stock, vinegar, sugar, salt, pepper, and red pepper flakes. Stir to combine. Cover and cook on low for 5 to 6 hours.

2. Transfer the ham bone to a cutting board and let it cool. When cool enough to handle, shred the meat from the bone. Discard the bone. Return the meat to the slow cooker and stir into the greens. Season with additional salt and pepper, as needed, before serving.

TIP: Make the greens vegetarian by removing the ham and using vegetable stock instead.

ARTICHOKE-PARMESAN DIP
WITH CROSTINI

SERVES 10

PREP
10 MINUTES

COOK
2 HOURS ON LOW

Cheesy, creamy, and a great option when serving a big party, this artichoke dip is easy to pull together in a pinch—especially since it's made from items you may mostly have on hand. Sometimes, I swap one can of artichokes for a 10-ounce box of thawed, drained, and wrung-out spinach, though you can use an equal amount of fresh greens from the garden as well.

1. Use the cooking spray or olive oil to coat the inside (bottom and sides) of the slow cooker. Pull any tough leaves from the artichokes and discard them. Add the artichokes, onion, mayonnaise, cream cheese, sour cream, garlic salt, pepper, red pepper flakes, mozzarella, Parmesan, and heavy cream to the slow cooker. Stir to combine. Cover and cook on low for 2 hours.

2. Season with additional garlic salt and pepper, as needed. Serve with the crostini.

TIP: The dip can also be served with crackers, such as Wheat Thins, or toasted pita.

Cooking spray or
1 tablespoon extra-virgin olive oil

2 (14-ounce) cans artichokes, drained

1 small onion, minced

½ cup mayonnaise

6 ounces cream cheese, at room temperature

¼ cup sour cream

½ teaspoon garlic salt, plus more for seasoning

¼ teaspoon freshly ground black pepper, plus more for seasoning

¼ teaspoon red pepper flakes

½ cup mozzarella cheese

⅓ cup grated Parmesan cheese

¼ cup heavy (whipping) cream

1 baguette, sliced and toasted, for crostini

Cooking spray or
1 tablespoon extra-virgin
olive oil

¾ cup mayonnaise

¼ cup bottled chili sauce

2 tablespoons ketchup

1 tablespoon pickle relish

½ teaspoon kosher salt,
plus more for seasoning

¼ teaspoon freshly ground
black pepper, plus more
for seasoning

2 tablespoons minced onion

2 cups Zesty Beef Brisket
(page 62) or store-bought,
chopped

1 (8-ounce) package
cream cheese, at room
temperature

2 cups shredded
Swiss cheese

1½ cups sauerkraut,
drained and chopped

1 package cocktail rye bread

REUBEN DIP

This easy, quick dip threatens to replace the
Reuben sandwich and corned beef and cabbage
as your St. Paddy's Day go-tos. I'll go on record, in
fact, to say I like it even better. Slathered on cocktail
rye or mini-pumpernickel bread, it's a party-ready
must-have that you'll also make just because.

1. Use the cooking spray or olive oil to coat the inside (bottom
and sides) of the slow cooker. In a medium bowl, combine the
mayonnaise, chili sauce, ketchup, relish, salt, pepper, and onion.
Put the mayonnaise mixture into the slow cooker, along with the
corned beef, cream cheese, Swiss cheese, and sauerkraut. Stir to
combine. Cover and cook on low for 1 hour, stirring occasionally.

2. Season with additional salt and pepper, as desired. Serve with
the rye bread.

TIP: The dip can be held on the warm setting for up to 2 hours.

BEAN DIP

SERVES 12

PREP
10 MINUTES

COOK
8 TO 10 HOURS
ON LOW

There's no reason to buy the preservative-packed bean dip you find on grocery store shelves; this is simple to make and definitely more enjoyable to eat. Plus, it's inexpensive to make and has all sorts of applications when it comes to leftovers—not that you're likely to have any.

1. Use the cooking spray or olive oil to coat the inside (bottom and sides) of the slow cooker. Add the beans, bacon, chili powder, salt, cumin, oregano, and water. Stir to combine. Cover and cook for 6 to 8 hours, or until the beans are tender when pierced with a fork. Add additional water by one-quarter cup at a time if the beans start to look dry.

2. About 2 hours before serving, mash the beans with a potato masher or the back of a fork, leaving some texture. Add the sour cream, cream cheese, salsa, and Cheddar. Stir to combine. Cover and continue cooking for another 2 hours.

3. Season with additional salt, as needed. Serve with the tortilla chips.

TIP: Use any leftovers, along with chopped red onion and sour cream, to make tasty bean burritos.

Cooking spray or
1 tablespoon extra-virgin
olive oil

1 pound dry pinto beans,
picked over, soaked
overnight, drained,
and rinsed

2 bacon slices, finely diced

1 tablespoon chili powder

1¼ teaspoons kosher salt,
plus more for seasoning

½ teaspoon ground cumin

½ teaspoon dried oregano

5 cups water, plus more if
beans start to look dry

¾ cup sour cream

1 (4-ounce) package
cream cheese

1 cup homemade or
store-bought salsa

2 cups shredded
Cheddar cheese

1 bag tortilla chips

1 pound ground beef

1 (1.25-ounce) package taco seasoning

1 (4-ounce) can diced green chiles

1 small onion, minced

1½ cups salsa, preferably chunky

1 pound processed cheese, cubed

1 cup sour cream

TACO DIP

Warm and gooey and waiting to be scooped up with crunchy tortilla chips, this taco dip is an ideal way to use up what's in the fridge. Have some fresh jalapeños? Use them to replace the chopped, canned chiles. Experiencing a bumper crop of veggies from the garden? Chop up some tomatoes, onions, cilantro, and hot peppers, and use them to make a quick homemade salsa to accompany, or even swirl into, the dip. And reach for that Velveeta or other processed cheese you've been hiding from company—it has a starring role to play here.

BROWN: In a slow cooker with a stove-top function, or in a Dutch oven or heavy-bottomed pan over medium-high heat, heat 1 tablespoon extra-virgin olive oil until shimmering. Add the beef and brown, breaking it up into small bits, until no pink remains.

If browned outside the slow cooker, place the beef in the slow cooker. Add the taco seasoning, chiles, onion, salsa, cheese, and sour cream. Stir to combine. Cover and cook on low for 2 to 3 hours. Serve while still warm and gooey.

TIP: This dip can be held on warm for up to 2 hours, making it a good option for a party or casual open house.

SOUTHERN-STYLE GREEN BEANS

SERVES 6

PREP
5 MINUTES

COOK
3 HOURS ON LOW

Typically, I prefer some crunch in my cooked veggies. However, these long-simmered green beans are the exception, with a sweet, smoky tang that can only be described as down-home delicious.

1. In the slow cooker, put the chicken stock, green beans, garlic, ham bone, butter, vinegar, sugar, all-purpose seasoning, salt, pepper, and garlic powder. Stir to mix. Cover and cook on low for 3 hours.

2. Season with additional salt and pepper, as needed. Serve.

TIP: The ham bone can be replaced with three bacon slices, preferably browned first and then crumbled into the dish before cooking begins.

2 cups Chicken Stock (page 30) or low-sodium if store-bought

1½ pounds fresh green beans, trimmed and snapped in half

1 garlic clove, minced

1 leftover ham bone (page 85)

2 tablespoons butter, cut into chunks

1 teaspoon white vinegar

1 teaspoon sugar

1 teaspoon all-purpose seasoning

½ teaspoon kosher salt, plus more for seasoning

½ teaspoon freshly ground black pepper, plus more for seasoning

½ teaspoon garlic powder

CREAMED KALE

Here in Chicago, creamed spinach is a steakhouse mainstay, right along with baked potatoes. However, it's not something I came around to until adulthood—I blame the old Popeye cartoons. Now that I'm officially a fan, I happen to think kale is a solid alternative, one that's sturdier and a tad more bitter. It stands up to the slow cooker better, too.

Cooking spray or
1 tablespoon extra-virgin olive oil

½ stick unsalted butter

2 garlic cloves, minced

½ cup heavy
(whipping) cream

2 ounces cream cheese

1½ cups whole milk

1 cup Chicken Stock
(page 30) or low-sodium if store-bought

4 tablespoons
all-purpose flour

½ cup finely grated
Parmesan cheese

½ teaspoon kosher salt, plus more for seasoning

½ teaspoon freshly ground black pepper, plus more for seasoning

¼ teaspoon ground nutmeg

¼ teaspoon red
pepper flakes

2 bunches kale, washed, stemmed, and leaves torn

1. If using a slow cooker with a stove-top function to make the sauce, first use the cooking spray or olive oil to coat the inside (bottom and sides) of the slow cooker. In the slow cooker or in a Dutch oven or heavy-bottomed pan over medium-high heat, prepare the sauce by whisking together the butter, garlic, whipping cream, cream cheese, milk, chicken stock, flour, and Parmesan until the butter and cheese are melted and the flour is incorporated, and the sauce is free of lumps.

2. If you prepared the sauce outside the slow cooker, use the cooking spray or olive oil to coat the inside (bottom and sides) of the slow cooker. Add the sauce to the slow cooker, along with the salt, pepper, nutmeg, red pepper flakes, and kale. Stir to combine. Cover and cook on low for 3 hours.

3. Season with additional salt and pepper, as needed. Serve.

TIP: You can replace the kale with most any green, such as collards or mustard greens. However, collards and mustard greens are more bitter and need a longer cooking time. Give them 45 minutes to 1 hour extra in the slow cooker.

MEASUREMENT CONVERSIONS

VOLUME EQUIVALENTS (LIQUID)

US STANDARD	US STANDARD (OUNCES)	METRIC (APPROXIMATE)
2 tablespoons	1 fl. oz.	30 mL
¼ cup	2 fl. oz.	60 mL
½ cup	4 fl. oz.	120 mL
1 cup	8 fl. oz.	240 mL
1½ cups	12 fl. oz.	355 mL
2 cups or 1 pint	16 fl. oz.	475 mL
4 cups or 1 quart	32 fl. oz.	1 L
1 gallon	128 fl. oz.	4 L

OVEN TEMPERATURES

FAHRENHEIT (F)	CELSIUS (C) (APPROXIMATE)
250°F	120°C
300°F	150°C
325°F	165°C
350°F	180°C
375°F	190°C
400°F	200°C
425°F	220°C
450°F	230°C

VOLUME EQUIVALENTS (DRY)

US STANDARD	METRIC (APPROXIMATE)
⅛ teaspoon	0.5 mL
¼ teaspoon	1 mL
½ teaspoon	2 mL
¾ teaspoon	4 mL
1 teaspoon	5 mL
1 tablespoon	15 mL
¼ cup	59 mL
⅓ cup	79 mL
½ cup	118 mL
⅔ cup	156 mL
¾ cup	177 mL
1 cup	235 mL
2 cups or 1 pint	475 mL
3 cups	700 mL
4 cups or 1 quart	1 L
½ gallon	2 L
1 gallon	4 L

WEIGHT EQUIVALENTS

US STANDARD	METRIC (APPROXIMATE)
½ ounce	15 g
1 ounce	30 g
2 ounces	60 g
4 ounces	115 g
8 ounces	225 g
12 ounces	340 g
16 ounces or 1 pound	455 g

RECIPE INDEX

INDEX

ACKNOWLEDGMENTS

I'd like to thank my family and friends who—from toddlerhood on—sampled my recipes, and supported and encouraged me. Thanks as well to my third grade teacher, Mrs. Gihring, who inspired me to write through the school of hard knocks. I'd also like to thank Callisto Media and my editor, Stacy Wagner-Kinnear, for the chance to compile this book of things that are near and dear.

ABOUT THE AUTHOR

Never one to be told, "Eat your veggies,"—or, frankly, meat—Jennifer Olvera wrote her first recipe on an index card when she could barely hold a pencil. As part of a lifelong quest to unveil food that defined places and experiences, she traveled the globe—from Haiti to South Africa, Australia to Spain, Peru, India, and Bora Bora—sampling ingredients and stuffing her suitcase with edible souvenirs along the way. As a longtime recipe developer, she penned a long-standing column for Serious Eats and features for the *Los Angeles Times, Chicago Tribune, Chicago Sun-Times,* and Frommers. com. This is her fourth book, among which is the definitive *Food Lovers' Guide to Chicago.*